OLD MOORE'S

se

2019 !!

Happy
New
year!

♡ mom

HOROSCOPE
AND ASTRAL
DIARY

LEO

OLD MOORE'S

HOROSCOPE AND ASTRAL DIARY

LEO

foulsham
LONDON • NEW YORK • TORONTO • SYDNEY

W. Foulsham & Co. Ltd
for Foulsham Publishing Ltd
The Old Barrel Store, Drayman's Lane, Marlow, Bucks SL7 2FF

Foulsham books can be found in all good bookshops and direct from
www.foulsham.com

ISBN: 978-0-572-04739-9

Copyright © 2018 Foulsham Publishing Ltd

A CIP record for this book is available from the British Library

Printed in Great Britain by Martins The Printers, Berwick-upon-Tweed

CONTENTS

INTRODUCTION

Astrology has been a part of life for centuries now, and no matter how technological our lives become, it seems that it never diminishes in popularity. For thousands of years people have been gazing up at the star-clad heavens and seeing their own activities and proclivities reflected in the movement of those little points of light. Across centuries countless hours have been spent studying the way our natures, activities and decisions seem to be paralleled by their predictable movements. Old Moore, a time-served veteran in astrological research, continues to monitor the zodiac and has produced the Astral Diary for 2019, tailor-made to your own astrological makeup.

Old Moore's Astral Diary is unique in its ability to get the heart of your nature and to offer you the sort of advice that might come from a trusted friend. It enables you to see in a day-by-day sense exactly how the planets are working for you. The diary section advises how you can get the best from upcoming situations and allows you to plan ahead successfully. There's also room on each daily entry to record your own observations or appointments.

While other popular astrology books merely deal with your astrological 'Sun sign', the Astral Diaries go much further. Every person on the planet is unique and Old Moore allows you to access your individuality in a number of ways. The front section gives you the chance to work out the placement of the Moon at the time of your birth and to see how its position has set an important seal on your overall nature. Perhaps most important of all, you can use the Astral Diary to discover your Rising Sign. This is the zodiac sign that was appearing over the Eastern horizon at the time of your birth and is just as important to you as an individual as is your Sun sign.

It is the synthesis of many different astrological possibilities that makes you what you are and with the Astral Diaries you can learn so much. How do you react to love and romance? Through the unique Venus tables and the readings that follow them, you can learn where the planet Venus was at the time of your birth. It is even possible to register when little Mercury is 'retrograde', which means that it appears to be moving backwards in space when viewed from the Earth. Mercury rules communication, so be prepared to deal with a few setbacks in this area when you see the sign ☿. The Astral Diary will be an interest and a support throughout the whole year ahead.

Old Moore extends his customary greeting to all people of the Earth and offers his age-old wishes for a happy and prosperous period ahead.

THE ESSENCE
OF LEO

Exploring the Personality of
Leo the Lion

(23RD JULY – 23RD AUGUST)

What's in a sign?

What really sets you apart from the herd is your naturally cheerful tendencies and your ability to display a noble and very brave face to the world at large. Leos are big people, no matter what their physical size may be and it is clear that you could never be an 'also-ran'. Quite the reverse is usually the case because you are at the forefront of many ventures, ideas and enterprises.

Being a Leo brings quite a few responsibilities. For example, people tend to look up to you, which means you have to be on your best behaviour for a lot of the time. Not that this prevents you from showing a slightly mischievous face to the world on a regular basis. You are not given to worrying too much because you generally know how to get yourself out of any sort of difficulty with ease. It's true that you tend to face problems head-on – a natural extension of your rather courageous temperament. Sometimes this can get you into unnecessary scrapes, as can your tendency to pit yourself against the forces of nature, or social groups that you feel to be absolutely wrong in their intentions or objectives.

As a Leo you do recognise that you have a responsibility to others, particularly those types who are shyer than you, or individuals who just don't have the ability to look after themselves. With a smile and a shrug you are inclined to put a protecting arm around the whole world. In effect you are the perfect big brother or sister and take pride in the position you tend to gain in society. In a work sense you are capable and can very easily find yourself in a situation of responsibility. You don't worry about this and can make a fine executive in almost any profession. There's no doubt though that you are naturally best placed at the head of things.

It's true that you are inclined to do too much and that your levels of energy are far from inexhaustible. However, it's a love of life that counts for the most in your case, and nothing is going to prevent you from being the happy, sunny, freewheeling soul that represents the sign of Leo at its very best.

Leo resources

Your ruling planet is the Sun, the source of all heat, light and therefore life on the Earth. The Sun is fundamental to our very existence, and its primary importance at the centre of things is reflected in your nature. Unlike your brother sign, Aries, you display your Fire-sign tendencies in a more controlled manner and without the need to dominate to such a great extent. All the same your natural position is at the head of things and this is reflected in the resources you draw from the zodiac.

One of your greatest gifts is a natural tendency to look confident, even on those occasions when you might be quaking inside. It's amazing what a difference this makes because it more or less ensures that others will trust you and tend to follow your lead. Once they do you rise to the occasion in an admirable way because you don't want to let your followers down. In almost any situation that life could present, you will quite naturally take charge, and those around you are invariably happy that it should be so.

Most Leos are capable in a practical as well as a theoretical way but a hands-on approach probably works best. Leo leads from the front, which means having to keep fit and healthy. This is vital, but like the lion that your sign represents you can get rather lethargic and flabby if you don't keep in shape. Also like the lion you do have a tendency to appear lazy on occasions, but only usually when things are already running smoothly around you.

The professions chosen by Leos are many and varied. It isn't really the subject matter that is important, merely your ability to make an impression. At work, as well as in social situations, you can shine like the very Sun that rules you. Usually well liked and respected, you are in a position to utilise the popularity that comes your way in order to feather your own nest, as well as those of people around you. Domestically speaking you have a great love of home and family, though you might tend to stifle those you love a little on occasions.

Beneath the surface

'What really makes me tick?' A fair question, and one that members of many zodiac signs are constantly inclined to ask themselves – but not you. The fact is that you are not the deepest thinker around. This is not to suggest that you don't have lofty ideals or a very sound moral base to your behaviour. The reason that you probably are not one of life's natural philosophers is because you are a 'doer'. In the time it takes others to mull over any given situation you will have sorted it out and moved on to the next task. However, this is a natural skill that can be honed to perfection and depends in part on getting yourself interested in the first place.

Your boredom threshold tends to be quite low and you would soon feel fatigued if you were forced to remain in situations which meant doing the same thing time and time again. Your driving, sometimes impatient mentality does demand change, and you can become irritable and out of sorts if you don't find it.

Are you as confident as you often appear to be? The answer to that one has to be yes. The fact is that you quite often fail to bear in mind the possibility of failure. Of course this means that you are more disappointed than most when things do go wrong, but your very conviction often leads to success. Once you do get down in the dumps however, you can be a very sorry picture indeed. Fortunately, you have the mental and spiritual reserves to pick yourself up fairly quickly and to push forward once again.

In matters of love you are probably more reserved than you give the impression of being. All the same you know how to deal with relationships – that is until you start acting like a lion again. The over-protective quality of your animal sign is always a danger, and one that you need to control. Perhaps here we find the Achilles heel of Leo. It is quite common for you to experience a sense of jealousy, a fact that would make you more possessive than usual. You have to remember that it's fine to love, but impossible to 'own' another individual.

In the main you offer the world an exterior smile that reflects your genuine inner state. Truthfulness shows on your face, and is usually felt in your heart in equal proportion.

Making the best of yourself

To feel good and to make the right sort of impression, you have to look good too. Nobody goes to the safari park to see a moth-eaten lion. You can dress cheaply, but you have to cut a dash in some way. Drab colours definitely don't suit your personality, with bright oranges and yellows being the most favoured – a reflection of your Sun rulership. Once you are properly attired you tend to move forward positively through life. Most Leos are quite attractive people, mainly because the honesty, frankness and genuine courage of your personality has a habit of finding its way to the surface.

There is one line of Kipling's famous poem 'If' that springs to mind as an object lesson for Leo, this being 'And yet don't look too good, nor talk too wise'. It is quite possible for you to go over the top in your enthusiasm and even courage isn't same thing as foolhardiness. A little humility can go a long way, as can a determination to learn from people who know better than you do. Constantly knocking your head against the same brick wall isn't very productive, and can sometimes be avoided by simply showing a willingness to take advice. And it isn't as if people are unwilling to lend a hand. The Leo subjects who achieve the most in life have learned how to co-operate, though without feeling that they are having to relinquish the leading position in life that is so important to them.

In order for you truly to make the best of yourself you also need to be fit. Leos are inclined to have some problems associated with the heart and the circulatory system, so you need to exercise regularly and to avoid the sort of constant stress that can lead to longer-term health difficulties. To most Leos laughter is the best tonic of all.

The impressions you give

If we could all genuinely see ourselves as others see us, how much easier would be our interaction with the world at large? Yours may not be the most intuitive sign of the zodiac but you are perceptive enough to know when you are giving the right impression. If this fact is sometimes obscured it is at least easy for you to monitor when things are not going right. In turn this should result in a slight modification of your own personality to take account of circumstances.

If you have any specific problem in this direction it stems from the fact that you are not a natural philosopher. Doing is far more important than thinking to you, a truism that can sometimes be your downfall. More attention to detail and a better appraisal of others allow you to offer a much better impression of yourself.

Most people already find you sunny, warm, frank, free, delightfully outspoken and very brave. All you have to do to achieve real success is to build on the qualities you already possess and to make allowance for the fact that the world is full of individuals. You can't browbeat others into liking you, even though popularity is important to you. There will always be people who don't take to your personality and there really isn't much you can do about the situation.

A great advantage for you is that it isn't difficult for you to appear to know what you are talking about, even when you don't. You can gain extra skills on the way and should use the very real magnetism of your personality both to help the world and to improve your own situation. Few people would find you easy either to dismiss or to forget, which can be another very definite advantage in life.

A sense of proportion is sometimes important, as well as a defined purpose in your statements and actions. All in all you have most of the components that allow you to be popular. Build on these and your true Leo worth will be there for all to see.

The way forward

No sign of the zodiac typifies its planetary ruler more than your own sign of Leo. When you smile, the Sun comes out and your laughter is so infectious that even the hardest-hearted types would be likely to smile themselves. Add to this the fact that you typify the statement 'fools rush in where angels fear to tread' and you have a formidable combination at your disposal. It might be the case that you fail to take account of some of your actions, but a good-humoured and intelligent attitude to life also allows you to get out of scrapes as easily as you get into them.

Cultivate your tendency to stick up for the underdog and don't get yourself into a position in life that means you constantly have to pay lip service to people who clearly don't know what they are doing. You can't stand incompetence, arrogance, cruelty or oppression. Of course this is a fine attitude, but you can't put the world right on your own, so once again co-operation proves to be the key to success.

In a career sense you need to be doing something that constantly stretches you. Your boredom threshold is not high and with constant tedium can come a worrisome streak and a tendency to health difficulties. Variety in work is the spice of your life, together with an active and useful social life, which is also vitally important.

In matters of love you are sincere and ardent, though with a tendency towards being a little too possessive. Allowing others the freedom to go their own way means finding more happiness yourself and lifts the noble qualities of your nature to new heights. Leos are still more likely than people from other zodiac signs to find one important relationship in life and to stick with it. Part of the reason for this state of affairs is that you have a horror of failure and will persist, even when others fall by the wayside.

You may not be creative in the generally accepted sense of the word but you have a good eye for colour and enjoy cheerful surroundings. Practical and capable, you won't need to call on the services of experts too often, since Leos generally don't shy away from DIY chores.

Diet is vitally important because as a Leo you are inclined to put on weight readily. Exercise helps here and is something you revel in anyway. Use your natural talents to the full, defend the weak and fight oppressors and you can't go far wrong in your life. Most important of all, keep smiling. You are tremendous fun to have around.

LEO ON THE CUSP

Old Moore is often asked how astrological profiles are altered for those people born at either the beginning or the end of a zodiac sign, or, more properly, on the cusps of a sign. In the case of Leo this would be on the 23rd of July and for two or three days after, and similarly at the end of the sign, probably from the 21st to the 23rd of August. In this year's Astral Diaries, once again, Old Moore sets out to explain the differences regarding cuspid signs.

The Cancer Cusp – July 23rd to July 25th

You tend to take life at a slower pace than Leo when taken on its own. You are more sensitive and quieter by nature, with slightly less drive and enthusiasm and a less dynamic disposition. With a creative and generally aspiring nature, you draw from Leo the fearless qualities that are typical of the sign, but these only tend to show on those occasions when you feel very strongly about things. There is quite a contradiction between these two signs and therefore you have a tendency to show very different faces in different circumstances. This fact makes you slightly awkward to predict and you often shock people as a result. Just when the world thinks it has you pigeon-holed, off you go at a tangent, perplexing your relatives and friends all over again. Family members are very important to you and when your aspiring and lofty qualities show most it is often on their behalf. In matters of love you tend to be very loyal, and have the ability to mix very well with others, enjoying cheerful and original people as part of your social circle.

One area that needs particular attention is your health. Although generally more robust than you probably give yourself credit for, you get through a tremendous amount of nervous energy, much more than others may realise. You need to watch your diet very carefully and to avoid acidic foods, which can upset your stomach. Apart from this, however, you are virtually indestructible and have the capacity to work long and hard to achieve your objectives.

At work you do your best to be adaptable and are very good at managing others. The natural frustrations of Leo, when faced with opposition, are less accented in your case. You have the ability to get on well and should make a mark for yourself when happy with your lot. Few would find you overbearing or bossy, although at times you seem to lack some of the natural Leo confidence. Most important of all though – you are kind, generous, trusting and very good to know.

The Virgo Cusp – August 21st to August 23rd

Perhaps the greatest difficulty for people born under the influence of this cusp is in making themselves understood. You probably think that you are the least complicated person in the world, but that isn't the way others see you. Your nature is full of contradictions. On the one hand you are fanatically tidy, and yet you can work in a state of almost total chaos; you love to travel and yet, deep inside, you are a home bird; and you talk a great deal, but often with quiet confidence. To disentangle all these contradictions is as difficult for you as it is for anyone else, and so you may often not reach the level of self-confidence that you deserve.

You have most of the positive qualities associated with the zodiac sign of Leo and your lofty, aspiring, sunny disposition is usually well accepted. Beneath this, however, is a quiet and contemplative person, who needs moments alone to synthesise the many happenings in a busy life. Usually physically robust, you do tend to worry more than is good for you, frequently about matters that are not particularly important. Meditation suits you well, particularly the kind that has a physical aspect, as this satisfies your Leo qualities, too. With a nervous system that varies from day to day, it is important for you to be sure that you achieve the level of relaxation that is vital to your Virgoan qualities. For you this could be anything between a crossword puzzle and two weeks on a cruise ship. In social settings you enjoy a degree of variety and can manage quite well with new people, even though you often tend to stick to people with whom you are familiar.

It's always important for you to keep an open mind and you shouldn't allow negative thoughts to build up. Keeping busy makes sense, as long as you don't continually choose to burn the candle at both ends. The people who know you the best do find you difficult to understand, but they are inclined to love you all the more for that. The most important character trait for you to cultivate is optimism because the more cheerful you remain regarding the future, the greater is the effort you expound upon it.

LEO AND ITS ASCENDANTS

The nature of every individual on the planet is composed of the rich variety of zodiac signs and planetary positions that were present at the time of their birth. Your Sun sign, which in your case is Leo, is one of the many factors when it comes to assessing the unique person you are. Probably the most important consideration, other than your Sun sign, is to establish the zodiac sign that was rising over the eastern horizon at the time that you were born. This is your Ascending or Rising sign. Most popular astrology fails to take account of the Ascendant, and yet its importance remains with you from the very moment of your birth, through every day of your life. The Ascendant is evident in the way you approach the world, and so, when meeting a person for the first time, it is this astrological influence that you are most likely to notice first. Our Ascending sign essentially represents what we appear to be, while the Sun sign is what we feel inside ourselves.

The Ascendant also has the potential for modifying our overall nature. For example, if you were born at a time of day when Leo was passing over the eastern horizon (this would be around the time of dawn) then you would be classed as a double Leo. As such, you would typify this zodiac sign, both internally and in your dealings with others. However, if your Ascendant sign turned out to be a Water sign, such as Pisces, there would be a profound alteration of nature, away from the expected qualities of Leo.

One of the reasons why popular astrology often ignores the Ascendant is that it has always been rather difficult to establish. Old Moore has found a way to make this possible by devising an easy-to-use table, which you will find on page 125 of this book. Using this, you can establish your Ascendant sign at a glance. You will need to know your rough time of birth, then it is simply a case of following the instructions.

For those readers who have no idea of their time of birth it might be worth allowing a good friend, or perhaps your partner, to read through the section that follows this introduction. Someone who deals with you on a regular basis may easily discover your Ascending sign, even though you could have some difficulty establishing it for yourself. A good understanding of this component of your nature is essential if you want to be aware of that 'other person' who is responsible for the way you make contact with the world at large. Your Sun sign, Ascendant sign, and the other pointers in this book will, together, allow you a far better understanding of what makes you tick as an individual. Peeling back the different layers of your astrological make-up can be an enlightening experience, and the Ascendant may represent one of the most important layers of all.

Leo with Leo Ascendant

This is a combination that could make even Old Moore breathless! The fact is that you are a go-getter of the first order, and there is virtually nothing in life that would prevent you from getting what you want. The problem here is that once you have it, you probably want something else. All in all you could end up like a dog chasing its own tail and so the first advice is to slow down and enjoy the journey a little more. Not that all of this makes you any less likeable, or indispensable, to a whole host of people. You smile much more often than you scowl and you won't make heavy weather of problems that would rock others back on their heels.

You are rather materialistic, and ultimate success probably means more to you than it should, but you can easily stop on your hectic journey to take note of those who have fallen by the wayside and give them a helping hand. If all that power is used for the good of humanity you might even become a living saint, except for the fact that you would be too busy to accept the honour. Be careful that you don't weigh yourself down with so many responsibilities that you fail to notice your progress, and travel as much as you can because this will certainly broaden your mind. Most people find you very attractive and fun to have around.

Leo with Virgo Ascendant

Here we have cheerfulness allied to efficiency, which can be a very positive combination for most of the time. With all the sense of honour, justice and bravery of the Leo subject, Virgo adds better staying power through tedious situations and offers you a slightly more serious view of life than we would expect from the Lion alone. In almost any situation you can keep going until you get to your chosen destination and you also find the time to reach out to the people who need your unique nature the most. Few would deny your kindness, though you can attract a little envy because it seems as though yours is the sort of personality that everyone else wants.

Most people born with this combination have a radiant smile and will do their utmost to think situations through carefully. If there is any tendency to be foolhardy, it is carefully masked beneath a covering of Virgoan common sense. Family matters are dealt with efficiently and with great love. Some might see you as close one moment and distant the next. The truth is that you are always on the go and have a thousand different things to think about, all at the same time. On the whole your presence is noticed, and you may represent the most loyal friend of them all.

Leo with Libra Ascendant

Libra brings slightly more flexibility to the fixed quality of the Leo nature. On the whole you do not represent a picture that is so very different from other versions of the Lion, though you find more time to smile, enjoy changing your mind a great deal more and have a greater number of casual friends. Few would find you proud or haughty and you retain the common touch that can be so important when it comes to getting on in life generally. At work you like to do something that brings variety, and would probably soon tire of doing the same task over and over again. Many of you are teachers, for you have patience, allied to a stubborn core. This can be an indispensable combination on occasions and is part of the reason for the material success that many folk with this combination achieve.

It isn't often that you get down in the dumps, as there is generally something more important around the next corner and you love the cut and thrust of everyday life. You always manage to stay young at heart, no matter what your age might be, and you revel in the company of interesting and stimulating types. Maybe you should try harder to concentrate on one thing at once and also strive to retain a serious opinion for more than ten minutes at a time, although Leo does help to control any flighty tendencies which show up.

Leo with Scorpio Ascendant

A Leo with intensity, that is what you are. You are committed to good causes and would argue the hind leg off a donkey in defence of your many ideals. If you are not out there saving the planet you could just be at home in the bath, thinking up the next way to save humanity from its own worst excesses. In your own life, although you love little luxuries, you are sparing and frugal, yet generous as can be to those you take to. It's a fact that you don't like everyone and of course the same is true in reverse. It might be easier for you to understand why you dislike others than to appreciate the reverse side of the coin, for your pride can be badly dented on occasions. Scorpio brings a tendency to have down spells, though the fact that Leo is also strongly represented in your nature should prevent them from becoming a regular part of your life.

It is important for you to learn how to forgive and forget, and there isn't much point in bearing a grudge because you are basically too noble to do so. If something goes wrong, kiss the situation goodbye and get on with the next interesting adventure, of which there are many in your life. Stop-start situations sometimes get in the way but there are plenty of people around who would be only too willing to lend a helping hand.

Leo with Sagittarius Ascendant

Above and beyond anything else you are naturally funny, and this is an aspect of your nature that will bring you intact through a whole series of problems that you manage to create for yourself. Chatty, witty, charming, kind and loving, you personify the best qualities of both these signs, whilst also retaining the Fire-sign ability to keep going, long after the rest of the party has gone home to bed. Being great fun to have around, you attract friends in the way that a magnet attracts iron filings. Many of these will be casual connections but there will always be a nucleus of deep, abiding attachments that may stay around you for most of your life.

You don't often suffer from fatigue, but on those occasions when you do there is ample reason to stay still for a while and simply take stock of situations. Routines are not your thing and you like to fill your life with variety. It's important to do certain things right, however, and staying power is something that comes with age, assisted by the fixed quality of Leo. Few would lock horns with you in an argument, which you always have to win. In a way you are a natural debator but you can sometimes carry things too far if you are up against a worthy opponent. Confidence is not lacking and you go with ease through situations that would cause many people to give up.

Leo with Capricorn Ascendant

What really sets you apart is your endless patience and determination to get where you want to go, no matter how long it takes you to do so. On the way there are many sub-plots in your life and a wealth of entertaining situations to keep you amused. Probably somewhat quieter than the average Leo, you still have the capacity to be the life and soul of the party on those occasions when it suits you to be so. Energy, when allied to persistence, is a powerful commodity and you have a great need to take on causes of one sort or another. Probably at your best when defending the rights of the oppressed, you take the protecting qualities of Leo to greater heights than almost anyone else who is touched by the idealistic and regal qualities of the sign. If arguments come into your life, you deal with them quickly and, in the main, wisely. Like most Capricorn types, you take to a few individuals who will play a part in your life for years on end.

Being a good family type, your partner and children are extremely important and you will lavish the same patience, determination and ultimate success on their behalf that you do when dealing with more remote situations. The fact is that you do not know any other way to behave and you are at your best when there is some mountain to climb.

Leo with Aquarius Ascendant

All associations with Aquarius bring originality, and you are no exception. You aspire to do your best most of the time, but manage to achieve your objectives in an infinitely amusing and entertaining way. Not that you set out to do so, because if you are an actor on the stage of life, it seems as though you are a natural one. There is nothing remotely pretentious about your breezy personality or your ability to occupy the centre of any stage. This analogy is quite appropriate because you probably like the theatre. Being in any situation when reality is suspended for a while suits you down to the ground, and in any case you may regularly ask yourself if you even recognise what reality is. Always asking questions, both of yourself and of the world at large, you soldier on relentlessly, though not to the exclusion of having a good time on the way.

Keeping to tried and tested paths is not your way. You are a natural trail-blazer who is full of good ideas and who has the energy to put them into practice. You care deeply for the people who play an important part in your life, but are wise enough to allow them the space they need in order to develop their own personalities along the way. Most people like you, many love you, and one or two think that you are the best thing since sliced bread.

Leo with Pisces Ascendant

You are a very sensitive soul, on occasions too much so for your own good. However, there is no better advocate for the rights of humanity than you, and you constantly do what you can to support the downtrodden and oppressed. Good causes are your thing and there are likely to be many in your life. You will probably find yourself pushed to the front of almost any enterprise of which you are a part because, despite the deeper qualities of Pisces, you are a natural leader. Even on those occasions when it feels as though you lack confidence, you manage to muddle through somehow, and your smile is as broad as the day. Few sign combinations are more loved than this one, mainly because you do not have a malicious bone in your body and will readily forgive and forget, which the Lion on its own often will not.

Although you are capable of acting on impulse, you do so from a deep sense of moral conviction, so that most of your endeavours are designed to suit other people too. They recognise this fact, and will push a great deal of support back in your direction. Even when you come across troubles in your life you manage to find ways to sort them out, and will invariably find something new to smile about on the way. Your sensitivity rating is massive and you can easily be moved to tears.

Leo with Aries Ascendant

Here we come upon a situation in which Leo is allied with another Fire sign. This creates a character that could appear to be typically Aries at first sight and in many ways it is, though there are subtle differences that should not be ignored. Although you have the standard Aries ability for getting things done, many of the tasks you do undertake will be for and on behalf of others. You can be proud, and on some occasions even haughty, and yet you are also regal in your bearing and honest to the point of absurdity. Nobody could doubt your sincerity,

21

and you have the soul of a poet combined with the bravery of a lion.

All of this is good, but it makes you rather difficult to approach, unless the person in question has first adopted a crouching and subservient attitude. Not that you would wish them to do so. It's simply that the impression you give and the motivation that underpins it are two quite different things. You are greatly respected, and in the case of those individuals who know your real nature, you are also deeply loved. But life would be much simpler if you didn't always have to fight the wars that those around you are happy to start. Relaxation is a word you don't really understand and you would be doing yourself a favour if you looked it up in a dictionary.

Leo with Taurus Ascendant

Oh dear, this can be rather a hedonistic combination. The trouble is that Taurus tends to have a great sense of what looks and feels right, whilst Leo, being a Cat, is inclined to preen itself on almost any occasion. The combination tends towards self-love, which is all too likely for someone who is perfect. But don't be too dispirited about these facts, because there is a great deal going for you in other ways. For a start you have one of the warmest hearts to be found anywhere, and you are so brave that others marvel at the courage you display. The mountains that you climb may not be of the large, rocky sort, but you manage to find plenty of pinnacles to scale all the same, and you invariably get to the top.

Routines might bore you a little more than would be the case with Taurus alone, but you don't mind being alone. Why should you? You are probably the nicest person you know! Thus if you were ever to be cast up on a deserted island you would people the place all on your own, and there would never be any crime, untidiness or arguments. Problems only arise when other people are involved. However, in social settings you are charming, good to know and full of ideas that really have legs. You preserve your youth well into middle age but at base you can tend to worry more than is good for you.

Leo with Gemini Ascendant

Many Gemini people think about doing great things, whilst those who enjoy a Leo Sun do much more than simply think. You have the intrepid qualities of Gemini, but you always keep a sense of humour and are especially good to be around. Bold and quite fearless, you are inclined to go where nobody has gone before, no matter if this is into a precarious business venture or up a mountain that has not been previously climbed. It is people such as you who first explored the world, and you love to know what lies around the next corner and over the far hill.

Kind and loving, you are especially loyal to your friends and would do almost anything on their behalf. As a result they show the greatest concern for you too. However, there are times when the Cat walks alone, and you are probably better at being on your own than would often be the case for the typical Gemini subject. In many way you are fairly self-contained and don't tend to get bored too much unless you are forced to do the same things time and time again. You have a great sense of fun, could talk to just about anyone and usually greet the world with a big smile.

Leo with Cancer Ascendant

This can be a very fortunate combination, for when seen at its best it brings all the concern and the natural caring qualities of Cancer, allied to the more dynamic and very brave face of Leo. Somehow there is a great deal of visible energy here but it manifests itself in a way that always shows a concern for the world at large. No matter what charitable works are going on in your district, it is likely that you will be involved in one way or another, and you relish the cut and thrust of life much more than the retiring side of Cancer would seem to do. You are quite capable of walking alone and don't really need the company of others for large chunks of the average day. However, when you are in social situations you fare very well and can usually be observed with a smile on your face.

Conversationally speaking you have sound, considered opinions and often represent the voice of steady wisdom when faced with a situation that calls for arbitration. In fact you will often be put in this situation and there is more than one politician and union representative who shares this undeniably powerful zodiac combination. Like all those associated with the sign of Cancer you love to travel and can make a meal out of your journeys, with brave, intrepid Leo lending a hand in the planning and the doing.

THE MOON AND THE PART IT PLAYS IN YOUR LIFE

In astrology the Moon is probably the single most important heavenly body after the Sun. Its unique position, as partner to the Earth on its journey around the solar system, means that the Moon appears to pass through the signs of the zodiac extremely quickly. The zodiac position of the Moon at the time of your birth plays a great part in personal character and is especially significant in the build-up of your emotional nature.

Sun Moon Cycles

The first lunar cycle deals with the part the position of the Moon plays relative to your Sun sign. I have made the fluctuations of this pattern easy for you to understand by means of a simple cyclic graph. It appears on the first page of each 'Your Month At A Glance', under the title 'Highs and Lows'. The graph displays the lunar cycle and you will soon learn to understand how its movements have a bearing on your level of energy and your abilities.

Your Own Moon Sign

Discovering the position of the Moon at the time of your birth has always been notoriously difficult because tracking the complex zodiac positions of the Moon is not easy. This process has been reduced to three simple stages with Old Moore's unique Lunar Tables. A breakdown of the Moon's zodiac positions can be found from page 28 onwards, so that once you know what your Moon Sign is, you can see what part this plays in the overall build-up of your personal character.

If you follow the instructions on the next page you will soon be able to work out exactly what zodiac sign the Moon occupied on the day that you were born and you can then go on to compare the reading for this position with those of your Sun sign and your Ascendant. It is partly the comparison between these three important positions that goes towards making you the unique individual you are.

HOW TO DISCOVER YOUR MOON SIGN

This is a three-stage process. You may need a pen and a piece of paper but if you follow the instructions below the process should only take a minute or so.

STAGE 1 First of all you need to know the Moon Age at the time of your birth. If you look at Moon Table 1, on page 26, you will find all the years between 1920 and 2018 down the left side. Find the year of your birth and then trace across to the right to the month of your birth. Where the two intersect you will find a number. This is the date of the New Moon in the month that you were born. You now need to count forward the number of days between the New Moon and your own birthday. For example, if the New Moon in the month of your birth was shown as being the 6th and you were born on the 20th, your Moon Age Day would be 14. If the New Moon in the month of your birth came after your birthday, you need to count forward from the New Moon in the previous month. If you were born in a Leap Year, remember to count the 29th February. You can tell if your birth year was a Leap Year if the last two digits can be divided by four. Whatever the result, jot this number down so that you do not forget it.

STAGE 2 Take a look at Moon Table 2 on page 27. Down the left hand column look for the date of your birth. Now trace across to the month of your birth. Where the two meet you will find a letter. Copy this letter down alongside your Moon Age Day.

STAGE 3 Moon Table 3 on page 27 will supply you with the zodiac sign the Moon occupied on the day of your birth. Look for your Moon Age Day down the left hand column and then for the letter you found in Stage 2. Where the two converge you will find a zodiac sign and this is the sign occupied by the Moon on the day that you were born.

Your Zodiac Moon Sign Explained

You will find a profile of all zodiac Moon Signs on pages 28 to 31, showing in yet another way how astrology helps to make you into the individual that you are. In each daily entry of the Astral Diary you can find the zodiac position of the Moon for every day of the year. This also allows you to discover your lunar birthdays. Since the Moon passes through all the signs of the zodiac in about a month, you can expect something like twelve lunar birthdays each year. At these times you are likely to be emotionally steady and able to make the sort of decisions that have real, lasting value.

Moon Table I

YEAR	JUN	JUL	AUG	YEAR	JUN	JUL	AUG	YEAR	JUN	JUL	AUG
1921	6	5	3	1954	1/30	29	28	1987	26	25	24
1922	25	24	22	1955	20	19	17	1988	14	13	12
1923	14	14	12	1956	8	8	6	1989	3	3	1/31
1924	2	2/31	30	1957	27	27	25	1990	22	22	20
1925	21	20	19	1958	17	16	15	1991	11	11	9
1926	10	9	8	1959	6	6	4	1992	1/30	29	28
1927	29	28	27	1960	24	24	22	1993	20	19	17
1928	18	17	16	1961	13	12	11	1994	9	8	7
1929	7	6	5	1962	2	1/31	30	1995	27	27	26
1930	26	25	24	1963	21	20	19	1996	17	15	14
1931	16	15	13	1964	10	9	7	1997	5	4	3
1932	4	3	2/31	1965	29	28	26	1998	24	23	22
1933	23	22	21	1966	18	17	16	1999	13	13	11
1934	12	11	10	1967	7	7	5	2000	2	1/31	29
1935	1/30	30	29	1968	26	25	24	2001	21	20	19
1936	19	18	17	1969	14	13	12	2002	10	9	8
1937	8	8	6	1970	4	4	2	2003	29	28	27
1938	27	27	25	1971	22	22	20	2004	16	16	15
1939	17	16	15	1972	11	11	9	2005	6	6	4
1940	6	5	4	1973	1/30	29	28	2006	26	25	23
1941	24	24	22	1974	20	19	17	2007	15	15	13
1942	13	13	12	1975	9	9	7	2008	4	3	1/31
1943	2	2	1/30	1976	27	27	25	2009	23	22	20
1944	20	20	18	1977	16	16	14	2010	12	12	10
1945	10	9	8	1978	5	5	4	2011	2	2/31	29
1946	29	28	26	1979	24	24	22	2012	19	19	17
1947	18	17	16	1980	13	12	11	2013	8	7	6
1948	7	6	5	1981	2	1/31	29	2014	27	25	24
1949	26	25	24	1982	21	20	19	2015	17	16	15
1950	15	15	13	1983	11	10	8	2016	4	4	2
1951	4	4	2	1984	29	28	26	2017	24	23	22
1952	22	22	20	1985	18	17	16	2018	13	13	11
1953	11	11	9	1986	7	7	5	2019	2/31	30	28

Table 2

DAY	JUL	AUG
1	R	U
2	R	U
3	S	V
4	S	V
5	S	V
6	S	V
7	S	V
8	S	V
9	S	V
10	S	V
11	S	V
12	S	V
13	T	V
14	T	W
15	T	W
16	T	W
17	T	W
18	T	W
19	T	W
20	T	W
21	T	W
22	T	W
23	T	W
24	U	X
25	U	X
26	U	X
27	U	X
28	U	X
29	U	X
30	U	X
31	U	X

Table 3

M/D	R	S	T	U	V	W	X
0	CA	CA	LE	LE	LE	LE	VI
1	CA	LE	LE	LE	VI	VI	VI
2	LE	LE	LE	VI	VI	VI	LI
3	LE	LE	VI	VI	VI	LI	LI
4	LE	VI	VI	LI	LI	LI	LI
5	VI	VI	LI	LI	LI	SC	SC
6	VI	LI	LI	LI	SC	SC	SC
7	LI	LI	LI	SC	SC	SA	SA
8	LI	LI	SC	SC	SC	SA	SA
9	SC	SC	SC	SA	SA	SA	SA
10	SC	SC	SA	SA	SA	CP	CP
11	SA	SA	SA	CP	CP	CP	CP
12	SA	SA	SA	CP	CP	AQ	AQ
13	SA	SA	CP	CP	CP	AQ	AQ
14	CP	CP	CP	AQ	AQ	AQ	PI
15	CP	CP	AQ	AQ	AQ	PI	PI
16	AQ	AQ	AQ	AQ	PI	PI	PI
17	AQ	AQ	AQ	PI	PI	PI	AR
18	AQ	AQ	PI	PI	PI	AR	AR
19	PI	PI	PI	PI	AR	AR	AR
20	PI	PI	AR	AR	AR	TA	TA
21	PI	AR	AR	AR	TA	TA	TA
22	AR	AR	AR	TA	TA	TA	GE
23	AR	AR	TA	TA	TA	GE	GE
24	AR	TA	TA	TA	GE	GE	GE
25	TA	TA	GE	GE	GE	CA	CA
26	TA	GE	GE	GE	CA	CA	CA
27	GE	GE	GE	CA	CA	CA	LE
28	GE	GE	CA	CA	CA	LE	LE
29	GE	CA	CA	CA	LE	LE	LE

AR = Aries, TA = Taurus, GE = Gemini, CA = Cancer, LE = Leo, VI = Virgo, LI = Libra, SC = Scorpio, SA = Sagittarius, CP = Capricorn, AQ = Aquarius, PI = Pisces

MOON SIGNS

Moon in Aries

You have a strong imagination, courage, determination and a desire to do things in your own way and forge your own path through life.

Originality is a key attribute; you are seldom stuck for ideas although your mind is changeable and you could take the time to focus on individual tasks. Often quick-tempered, you take orders from few people and live life at a fast pace. Avoid health problems by taking regular time out for rest and relaxation.

Emotionally, it is important that you talk to those you are closest to and work out your true feelings. Once you discover that people are there to help, there is less necessity for you to do everything yourself.

Moon in Taurus

The Moon in Taurus gives you a courteous and friendly manner, which means you are likely to have many friends.

The good things in life mean a lot to you, as Taurus is an Earth sign that delights in experiences which please the senses. Hence you are probably a lover of good food and drink, which may in turn mean you need to keep an eye on the bathroom scales, especially as looking good is also important to you.

Emotionally you are fairly stable and you stick by your own standards. Taureans do not respond well to change. Intuition also plays an important part in your life.

Moon in Gemini

You have a warm-hearted character, sympathetic and eager to help others. At times reserved, you can also be articulate and chatty: this is part of the paradox of Gemini, which always brings duplicity to the nature. You are interested in current affairs, have a good intellect, and are good company and likely to have many friends. Most of your friends have a high opinion of you and would be ready to defend you should the need arise. However, this is usually unnecessary, as you are quite capable of defending yourself in any verbal confrontation.

Travel is important to your inquisitive mind and you find intellectual stimulus in mixing with people from different cultures. You also gain much from reading, writing and the arts but you do need plenty of rest and relaxation in order to avoid fatigue.

Moon in Cancer

The Moon in Cancer at the time of birth is a fortunate position as Cancer is the Moon's natural home. This means that the qualities of compassion and understanding given by the Moon are especially enhanced in your nature, and you are friendly and sociable and cope well with emotional pressures. You cherish home and family life, and happily do the domestic tasks. Your surroundings are important to you and you hate squalor and filth. You are likely to have a love of music and poetry.

Your basic character, although at times changeable like the Moon itself, depends on symmetry. You aim to make your surroundings comfortable and harmonious, for yourself and those close to you.

Moon in Leo

The best qualities of the Moon and Leo come together to make you warmhearted, fair, ambitious and self-confident. With good organisational abilities, you invariably rise to a position of responsibility in your chosen career. This is fortunate as you don't enjoy being an 'also-ran' and would rather be an important part of a small organisation than a menial in a large one.

You should be lucky in love, and happy, provided you put in the effort to make a comfortable home for yourself and those close to you. It is likely that you will have a love of pleasure, sport, music and literature. Life brings you many rewards, most of them as a direct result of your own efforts, although you may be luckier than average and ready to make the best of any situation.

Moon in Virgo

You are endowed with good mental abilities and a keen receptive memory, but you are never ostentatious or pretentious. Naturally quite reserved, you still have many friends, especially of the opposite sex. Marital relationships must be discussed carefully and worked at so that they remain harmonious, as personal attachments can be a problem if you do not give them your full attention.

Talented and persevering, you possess artistic qualities and are a good homemaker. Earning your honours through genuine merit, you work long and hard towards your objectives but show little pride in your achievements. Many short journeys will be undertaken in your life.

Moon in Libra

With the Moon in Libra you are naturally popular and make friends easily. People like you, probably more than you realise, you bring fun to a party and are a natural diplomat. For all its good points, Libra is not the most stable of astrological signs and, as a result, your emotions can be a little unstable too. Therefore, although the Moon in Libra is said to be good for love and marriage, your Sun sign and Rising sign will have an important effect on your emotional and loving qualities.

You must remember to relate to others in your decision-making. Co-operation is crucial because Libra represents the 'balance' of life that can only be achieved through harmonious relationships. Conformity is not easy for you because Libra, an Air sign, likes its independence.

Moon in Scorpio

Some people might call you pushy. In fact, all you really want to do is to live life to the full and protect yourself and your family from the pressures of life. Take care to avoid giving the impression of being sarcastic or impulsive and use your energies wisely and constructively.

You have great courage and you invariably achieve your goals by force of personality and sheer effort. You are fond of mystery and are good at predicting the outcome of situations and events. Travel experiences can be beneficial to you.

You may experience problems if you do not take time to examine your motives in a relationship, and also if you allow jealousy, always a feature of Scorpio, to cloud your judgement.

Moon in Sagittarius

The Moon in Sagittarius helps to make you a generous individual with humanitarian qualities and a kind heart. Restlessness may be intrinsic as your mind is seldom still. Perhaps because of this, you have a need for change that could lead you to several major moves during your adult life. You are not afraid to stand your ground when you know your judgement is right, you speak directly and have good intuition.

At work you are quick, efficient and versatile and so you make an ideal employee. You need work to be intellectually demanding and do not enjoy tedious routines.

In relationships, you anger quickly if faced with stupidity or deception, though you are just as quick to forgive and forget. Emotionally, there are times when your heart rules your head.

Moon in Capricorn

The Moon in Capricorn makes you popular and likely to come into the public eye in some way. The watery Moon is not entirely comfortable in the Earth sign of Capricorn and this may lead to some difficulties in the early years of life. An initial lack of creative ability and indecision must be overcome before the true qualities of patience and perseverance inherent in Capricorn can show through.

You have good administrative ability and are a capable worker, and if you are careful you can accumulate wealth. But you must be cautious and take professional advice in partnerships, as you are open to deception. You may be interested in social or welfare work, which suit your organisational skills and sympathy for others.

Moon in Aquarius

The Moon in Aquarius makes you an active and agreeable person with a friendly, easy-going nature. Sympathetic to the needs of others, you flourish in a laid-back atmosphere. You are broad-minded, fair and open to suggestion, although sometimes you have an unconventional quality which others can find hard to understand.

You are interested in the strange and curious, and in old articles and places. You enjoy trips to these places and gain much from them. Political, scientific and educational work interests you and you might choose a career in science or technology.

Money-wise, you make gains through innovation and concentration and Lunar Aquarians often tackle more than one job at a time. In love you are kind and honest.

Moon in Pisces

You have a kind, sympathetic nature, somewhat retiring at times, but you always take account of others' feelings and help when you can.

Personal relationships may be problematic, but as life goes on you can learn from your experiences and develop a better understanding of yourself and the world around you.

You have a fondness for travel, appreciate beauty and harmony and hate disorder and strife. You may be fond of literature and would make a good writer or speaker yourself. You have a creative imagination and may come across as an incurable romantic. You have strong intuition, maybe bordering on a mediumistic quality, which sets you apart from the mass. You may not be rich in cash terms, but your personal gifts are worth more than gold.

LEO IN LOVE

Discover how compatible in love you are with people from the same and other signs of the zodiac. Five stars equals a match made in heaven!

Leo meets Leo

More of a mutual appreciation society than a relationship, this is a promising match. Leo is kind, considerate, lofty, idealistic and brave, all qualities which are mirrored by a Leo partner. Both Lions will be determined in their ambitions, recognise the importance of the family and share a mutual love in all areas of their lives. Furthermore, Leo loves to be loved and so will give and receive it in equal amounts. There won't be many arguments but when there are – watch out! Star rating: *****

Leo meets Virgo

There is a chance for this couple, but it won't be trouble-free. Leo and Virgo view life very differently: Virgo is of a serious nature, struggling to relate to Leo's relentless optimism and cheerfulness, and even finding it annoying. Leo, meanwhile, may find Virgo stodgy, sometimes dark, and uninspiring. The saving grace comes through communication – Leo knows how to make Virgo talk, which is what it needs. If this pair find happiness, though, it may be a case of opposites attract! Star rating: ***

Leo meets Libra

The biggest drawback here is likely to be in the issue of commitment. Leo knows everything about constancy and faithfulness, a lesson which, sadly, Libra needs to learn. Librans are easy-going and diplomatic, qualities which are useful when Leo is on the war-path. This couple should be compatible on a personal level and any problems tend to relate to the different way in which these signs deal with outside factors. With good will and an open mind, it can work out well enough. Star rating: ***

Leo meets Scorpio

Stand back and watch the sparks fly! Scorpio has the deep sensitivity of a Water sign but it is also partially ruled by Fire planet Mars, from which it draws a great power that Leo will find difficult. Leo loves to take charge and really hates to feel psychologically undermined, which is Scorpio's stock-in-trade. Scorpio may find Leo's ideals a little shallow, which will be upsetting to the Lion. Anything is possible, but this possibility is rather slimmer than most. Star rating: **

Leo meets Sagittarius

An excellent match, as Leo and Sagittarius have so much in common. Their general approach to life is very similar, although as they are both Fire signs they can clash impressively! Sagittarius is shallower and more flippant than Leo likes to think of itself, and the Archer will be the one taking emotional chances. Sagittarius has met its match in the Lion's den, as brave Leo won't be outdone by anyone. Financially, they will either be very wealthy or struggling, and family life may be chaotic. Problems, like joys, are handled jointly – and that leads to happiness. Star rating: *****

Leo meets Capricorn

Despite promising appearances, this match often fails to thrive. Capricorn focuses on long-term objectives and, like Leo, is very practical. Both signs are capable of attaining success after a great struggle, which while requiring effort, gives them a mutual goal. But when life is easier, the cracks begin to show. Capricorn can be too serious for Leo, and the couple share few ideals. Leo loves luxury, Capricorn seeks austerity. Leo is warm but Capricorn seems cold and wintry in comparison. Both have many good points, but they don't seem to fire each other off properly. Star rating: **

Leo meets Aquarius

The problem here is that Aquarius doesn't 'think' in the general sense of the word, it 'knows'. Leo, on the other hand, is more practical and relies more on logical reasoning, and consequently it doesn't understand Aquarius very well. Aquarians can also appear slightly frosty in their appreciation of others and this, too, will eventually annoy Leo. This is a good match for a business partnership because Aquarius is astute, while Leo is brave, but personally the prognosis is less promising. Tolerance, understanding and forbearance are all needed to make this work. Star rating: **

Leo meets Pisces *Annika*

Pisces always needs to understand others, which makes Leo feel warm and loved, while Leo sees, to its delight, that Pisces needs to be protected and taken care of. Pisceans are often lacking in self-confidence, which is something Leo has to spare, and happily it is often infectious. Pisces' inevitable cares are swept away on a tide of Leonine cheerfulness. This couple's home would be cheerful, and full of love which is beneficial to all family members. This is not a meeting of minds, but rather an understanding and appreciation of differences. Star rating: ****

Leo meets Aries *Sammie*

Stand by for action and make sure that the house is sound-proof! Leo is a lofty idealist and there is always likely to be friction when two Fire signs meet. To compensate, there is much mutual admiration, together with a desire to please. Where there are shared incentives, the prognosis is good but it's important not to let little irritations blow up. Both signs want to have their own way and this is a sure cause of trouble. There might not be much patience here, but there is plenty of action. Star rating: *****

Leo meets Taurus

Here we find a generally successful pairing, which frequently leads to an enduring relationship. Taurus needs stimulation which Leo is happy to offer, while Leo responds well to the Bull's sense of order. The essence of the relationship is balance, but it may be achieved with wild swings of the scales on the way, so don't expect a quiet life, though this pair will enjoy a reconciliation after an argument! Material success is probable and, as both like children, a family is likely. Star rating: ***

Leo meets Gemini

There can be problems here, but Gemini is adaptable enough to overcome many of them. Leo is a go-getter and might sometimes rail against Gemini's flighty tendencies, while Gemini's mental disorganisation can undermine Leo's practicality. However, Leo is cheerful and enjoys Gemini's jokey, flippant qualities. At times of personal intimacy, the two signs should be compatible. Leo and Gemini share very high ideals, but Leo will stick at them for longer. Patience is needed on both sides for the relationship to develop. Star rating: ***

Leo meets Cancer

This relationship will usually be directed by dominant Leo more towards its own needs than Cancer's. However, the Crab will willingly play second fiddle to more progressive and bossy types as it is deeply emotional and naturally supportive. Leo is bright, caring, magnanimous and protective and so, as long as it isn't over-assertive, this could be a good match. On the surface, Cancer appears the more conventional of the two, but Leo will discover, to its delight, that underneath it can be unusual and quirky. Star rating: ****

VENUS:
THE PLANET OF LOVE

If you look up at the sky around sunset or sunrise you will often see Venus in close attendance to the Sun. It is arguably one of the most beautiful sights of all and there is little wonder that historically it became associated with the goddess of love. But although Venus does play an important part in the way you view love and in the way others see you romantically, this is only one of the spheres of influence that it enjoys in your overall character.

Venus has a part to play in the more cultured side of your life and has much to do with your appreciation of art, literature, music and general creativity. Even the way you look is responsive to the part of the zodiac that Venus occupied at the start of your life, though this fact is also down to your Sun sign and Ascending sign. If, at the time you were born, Venus occupied one of the more gregarious zodiac signs, you will be more likely to wear your heart on your sleeve, as well as to be more attracted to entertainment, social gatherings and good company. If on the other hand Venus occupied a quiet zodiac sign at the time of your birth, you would tend to be more retiring and less willing to shine in public situations.

It's good to know what part the planet Venus plays in your life, for it can have a great bearing on the way you appear to the rest of the world and since we all have to mix with others, you can learn to make the very best of what Venus has to offer you.

One of the great complications in the past has always been trying to establish exactly what zodiac position Venus enjoyed when you were born, because the planet is notoriously difficult to track. However, I have solved that problem by creating a table that is exclusive to your Sun sign, which you will find on the following page.

Establishing your Venus sign could not be easier. Just look up the year of your birth on the page opposite and you will see a sign of the zodiac. This was the sign that Venus occupied in the period covered by your sign in that year. If Venus occupied more than one sign during the period, this is indicated by the date on which the sign changed, and the name of the new sign. For instance, if you were born in 1970, Venus was in Virgo until the 8th August, after which time it was in Libra. If you were born before 8th August your Venus sign is Virgo, if you were born on or after 8th August, your Venus sign is Libra. Once you have established the position of Venus at the time of your birth, you can then look in the pages which follow to see how this has a bearing on your life as a whole.

1921 GEMINI / 6.8 CANCER
1922 VIRGO / 11.8 LIBRA
1923 CANCER / 4.8 LEO
1924 GEMINI / 25.7 CANCER
1925 LEO / 28.7 VIRGO
1926 LEO / 24.7 VIRGO /
    18.8 LIBRA
1927 VIRGO
1928 LEO / 12.8 VIRGO
1929 GEMINI / 5.8 CANCER
1930 VIRGO / 10.8 LIBRA
1931 CANCER / 3.8 LEO
1932 GEMINI / 28.7 CANCER
1933 LEO / 27.7 VIRGO
1934 LEO / 23.7 VIRGO /
    17.8 LIBRA
1935 VIRGO
1936 LEO / 11.8 VIRGO
1937 GEMINI / 5.8 CANCER
1938 VIRGO / 10.8 LIBRA
1939 CANCER / 3.8 LEO
1940 GEMINI / 1.8 CANCER
1941 LEO / 27.7 VIRGO
1942 LEO / 23.7 VIRGO /
    17.8 LIBRA
1943 VIRGO
1944 LEO / 11.8 VIRGO
1945 GEMINI / 5.8 CANCER
1946 VIRGO / 9.8 LIBRA
1947 CANCER / 2.8 LEO
1948 GEMINI / 3.8 CANCER
1949 LEO / 26.7 VIRGO
1950 LEO / 23.7 VIRGO /
    16.8 LIBRA
1951 VIRGO
1952 LEO / 10.8 VIRGO
1953 GEMINI / 4.8 CANCER
1954 VIRGO / 9.8 LIBRA
1955 CANCER / 1.8 LEO
1956 GEMINI / 4.8 CANCER
1957 LEO / 26.7 VIRGO
1958 VIRGO / 16.8 LIBRA
1959 VIRGO
1960 LEO / 9.8 VIRGO
1961 GEMINI / 4.8 CANCER
1962 VIRGO / 9.8 LIBRA
1963 CANCER / 1.8 LEO
1964 GEMINI / 5.8 CANCER
1965 LEO / 25.7 VIRGO
1966 VIRGO / 16.8 LIBRA
1967 VIRGO
1968 LEO / 9.8 VIRGO
1969 GEMINI / 4.8 CANCER
1970 VIRGO / 8.8 LIBRA
1971 CANCER / 31.7 LEO
1972 GEMINI / 5.8 CANCER
1973 LEO / 25.7 VIRGO
1974 VIRGO / 15.8 LIBRA
1975 VIRGO

1976 LEO / 9.8 VIRGO
1977 GEMINI / 3.8 CANCER
1978 VIRGO / 8.8 LIBRA
1979 CANCER / 31.7 LEO
1980 GEMINI / 6.8 CANCER
1981 LEO / 24.7 VIRGO
1982 VIRGO / 15.8 LIBRA
1983 VIRGO
1984 LEO / 8.8 VIRGO
1985 GEMINI / 3.8 CANCER
1986 VIRGO / 7.8 LIBRA
1987 CANCER / 30.7 LEO
1988 GEMINI / 6.8 CANCER
1989 LEO / 24.7 VIRGO
1990 VIRGO / 14.8 LIBRA
1991 VIRGO / 22.8 LEO
1992 LEO / 8.8 VIRGO
1993 GEMINI / 2.8 CANCER
1994 VIRGO / 7.8 LIBRA
1995 CANCER / 30.7 LEO
1996 GEMINI / 7.8 CANCER
1997 LEO / 24.7 VIRGO
1998 VIRGO / 14.8 LIBRA
1999 VIRGO / 22.8 LEO
2000 LEO / 8.8 VIRGO
2001 GEMINI / 1.8 CANCER
2002 VIRGO / 8.8 LIBRA
2003 CANCER / 30.7 LEO
2004 GEMINI / 7.8 CANCER
2005 LEO / 24.7 VIRGO
2006 VIRGO / 14.8 LIBRA
2007 VIRGO / 22.8 LEO
2008 LEO / 8.8 VIRGO
2009 GEMINI / 1.8 CANCER
2010 VIRGO / 8.8 LIBRA
2011 CANCER / 30.7 LEO
2012 GEMINI / 7.8 CANCER
2013 LEO / 24.7 VIRGO
2014 VIRGO / 14.8 LIBRA
2015 VIRGO / 22.8 LEO
2016 LEO / 6.8 VIRGO
2017 GEMINI / 1.8 CANCER
2018 VIRGO / 8.8 LIBRA
2019 CANCER / 6.8 LEO

VENUS THROUGH THE ZODIAC SIGNS

Venus in Aries

Amongst other things, the position of Venus in Aries indicates a fondness for travel, music and all creative pursuits. Your nature tends to be affectionate and you would try not to create confusion or difficulty for others if it could be avoided. Many people with this planetary position have a great love of the theatre, and mental stimulation is of the greatest importance. Early romantic attachments are common with Venus in Aries, so it is very important to establish a genuine sense of romantic continuity. Early marriage is not recommended, especially if it is based on sympathy. You may give your heart a little too readily on occasions.

Venus in Taurus

You are capable of very deep feelings and your emotions tend to last for a very long time. This makes you a trusting partner and lover, whose constancy is second to none. In life you are precise and careful and always try to do things the right way. Although this means an ordered life, which you are comfortable with, it can also lead you to be rather too fussy for your own good. Despite your pleasant nature, you are very fixed in your opinions and quite able to speak your mind. Others are attracted to you and historical astrologers always quoted this position of Venus as being very fortunate in terms of marriage. However, if you find yourself involved in a failed relationship, it could take you a long time to trust again.

Venus in Gemini

As with all associations related to Gemini, you tend to be quite versatile, anxious for change and intelligent in your dealings with the world at large. You may gain money from more than one source but you are equally good at spending it. There is an inference here that you are a good communicator, via either the written or the spoken word, and you love to be in the company of interesting people. Always on the look-out for culture, you may also be very fond of music, and love to indulge the curious and cultured side of your nature. In romance you tend to have more than one relationship and could find yourself associated with someone who has previously been a friend or even a distant relative.

Venus in Cancer

You often stay close to home because you are very fond of family and enjoy many of your most treasured moments when you are with those you love. Being naturally sympathetic, you will always do anything you can to support those around you, even people you hardly know at all. This charitable side of your nature is your most noticeable trait and is one of the reasons why others are naturally so fond of you. Being receptive and in some cases even psychic, you can see through to the soul of most of those with whom you come into contact. You may not commence too many romantic attachments but when you do give your heart, it tends to be unconditionally.

Venus in Leo

It must become quickly obvious to almost anyone you meet that you are kind, sympathetic and yet determined enough to stand up for anyone or anything that is truly important to you. Bright and sunny, you warm the world with your natural enthusiasm and would rarely do anything to hurt those around you, or at least not intentionally. In romance you are ardent and sincere, though some may find your style just a little overpowering. Gains come through your contacts with other people and this could be especially true with regard to romance, for love and money often come hand in hand for those who were born with Venus in Leo. People claim to understand you, though you are more complex than you seem.

Venus in Virgo

Your nature could well be fairly quiet no matter what your Sun sign might be, though this fact often manifests itself as an inner peace and would not prevent you from being basically sociable. Some delays and even the odd disappointment in love cannot be ruled out with this planetary position, though it's a fact that you will usually find the happiness you look for in the end. Catapulting yourself into romantic entanglements that you know to be rather ill-advised is not sensible, and it would be better to wait before you committed yourself exclusively to any one person. It is the essence of your nature to serve the world at large and through doing so it is possible that you will attract money at some stage in your life.

Venus in Libra

Venus is very comfortable in Libra and bestows upon those people who have this planetary position a particular sort of kindness that is easy to recognise. This is a very good position for all sorts of friendships and also for romantic attachments that usually bring much joy into your life. Few individuals with Venus in Libra would avoid marriage and since you are capable of great depths of love, it is likely that you will find a contented personal life. You like to mix with people of integrity and intelligence but don't take kindly to scruffy surroundings or work that means getting your hands too dirty. Careful speculation, good business dealings and money through marriage all seem fairly likely.

Venus in Scorpio

You are quite open and tend to spend money quite freely, even on those occasions when you don't have very much. Although your intentions are always good, there are times when you get yourself in to the odd scrape and this can be particularly true when it comes to romance, which you may come to late or from a rather unexpected direction. Certainly you have the power to be happy and to make others contented on the way, but you find the odd stumbling block on your journey through life and it could seem that you have to work harder than those around you. As a result of this, you gain a much deeper understanding of the true value of personal happiness than many people ever do, and are likely to achieve true contentment in the end.

Venus in Sagittarius

You are lighthearted, cheerful and always able to see the funny side of any situation. These facts enhance your popularity, which is especially high with members of the opposite sex. You should never have to look too far to find romantic interest in your life, though it is just possible that you might be too willing to commit yourself before you are certain that the person in question is right for you. Part of the problem here extends to other areas of life too. The fact is that you like variety in everything and so can tire of situations that fail to offer it. All the same, if you choose wisely and learn to understand your restless side, then great happiness can be yours.

Venus in Capricorn

The most notable trait that comes from Venus in this position is that it makes you trustworthy and able to take on all sorts of responsibilities in life. People are instinctively fond of you and love you all the more because you are always ready to help those who are in any form of need. Social and business popularity can be yours and there is a magnetic quality to your nature that is particularly attractive in a romantic sense. Anyone who wants a partner for a lover, a spouse and a good friend too would almost certainly look in your direction. Constancy is the hallmark of your nature and unfaithfulness would go right against the grain. You might sometimes be a little too trusting.

Venus in Aquarius

This location of Venus offers a fondness for travel and a desire to try out something new at every possible opportunity. You are extremely easy to get along with and tend to have many friends from varied backgrounds, classes and inclinations. You like to live a distinct sort of life and gain a great deal from moving about, both in a career sense and with regard to your home. It is not out of the question that you could form a romantic attachment to someone who comes from far away or be attracted to a person of a distinctly artistic and original nature. What you cannot stand is jealousy, for you have friends of both sexes and would want to keep things that way.

Venus in Pisces

The first thing people tend to notice about you is your wonderful, warm smile. Being very charitable by nature you will do anything to help others, even if you don't know them well. Much of your life may be spent sorting out situations for other people, but it is very important to feel that you are living for yourself too. In the main, you remain cheerful, and tend to be quite attractive to members of the opposite sex. Where romantic attachments are concerned, you could be drawn to people who are significantly older or younger than yourself or to someone with a unique career or point of view. It might be best for you to avoid marrying whilst you are still very young.

HOW THE DIAGRAMS WORK

Through the picture diagrams in the Astral Diary I want to help you to plot your year. With them you can see where the positive and negative aspects will be found in each month. To make the most of them, all you have to do is remember where and when!

Let me show you how they work ...

THE MONTH AT A GLANCE

Just as there are twelve separate zodiac signs, so astrologers believe that each sign has twelve separate aspects to life. Each of the twelve segments relates to a different personal aspect. I list them all every month so that their meanings are always clear.

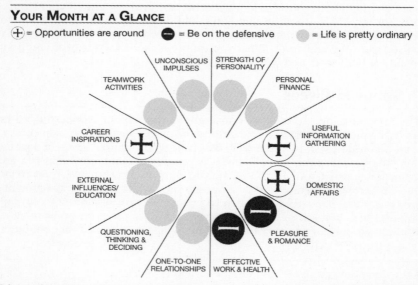

YOUR MONTH AT A GLANCE

⊕ = Opportunities are around   ⊖ = Be on the defensive   ○ = Life is pretty ordinary

UNCONSCIOUS IMPULSES — STRENGTH OF PERSONALITY — TEAMWORK ACTIVITIES — PERSONAL FINANCE — CAREER INSPIRATIONS — USEFUL INFORMATION GATHERING — EXTERNAL INFLUENCES/ EDUCATION — DOMESTIC AFFAIRS — QUESTIONING, THINKING & DECIDING — PLEASURE & ROMANCE — ONE-TO-ONE RELATIONSHIPS — EFFECTIVE WORK & HEALTH

I have designed this chart to show you how and when these twelve different aspects are being influenced throughout the year. When there is a shaded circle, nothing out of the ordinary is to be expected. However, when a circle turns white with a plus sign, the influence is positive. Where the circle is black with a minus sign, it is a negative.

42

YOUR ENERGY RHYTHM CHART

Below is a picture diagram in which I link your zodiac group to the rhythm of the Moon. In doing this I have calculated when you will be gaining strength from its influence and equally when you may be weakened by it.

If you think of yourself as being like the tides of the ocean then you may understand how your own energies must also rise and fall. And if you understand how it works and when it is working, then you can better organise your activities to achieve more and get things done more easily.

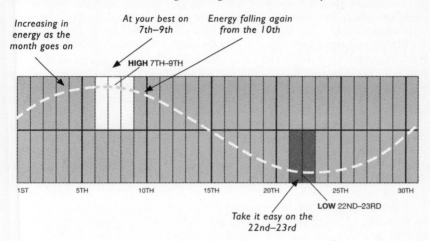

THE KEY DAYS

Some of the entries are in **bold**, which indicates the working of astrological cycles in your life. Look out for them each week as they are the best days to take action or make decisions. The daily text tells you which area of your life to focus on.

MERCURY RETROGRADE

The Mercury symbol (☿) indicates that Mercury is retrograde on that day. Since Mercury governs communication, the fact that it appears to be moving backwards when viewed from the Earth at this time should warn you that your communication skills are not likely to be at their best and you could expect some setbacks.

LEO: YOUR
YEAR IN BRIEF

At the start of the year, January and February should find you in an easy-going mood, a happy situation for you and the people with whom you spend most of your time. At work you come up with great ideas and set a good example in any team you are in. Money matters can be variable but when it matters the most you should have what you need, and maybe just a little extra on top.

March and April look steady and both months should offer you more of what you need in a material sense. There is some doubt as to whether you will get everything you require from an emotional point of view and you might have to work hard to gain the support you think is missing. Friends might prove to be more reliable than some relatives, but with a little trust you can make things right.

Early summer should be a moderately successful period for most Leos. During May and June you might not have quite the same verve as you showed at the start of the year but you are more relaxed and will find it easier to go with the flow. In a creative mood, this would be an ideal time for some major DIY or even for a possible house move. Travel seems most likely in June.

July and August are often a time for travel and this is certainly likely to be the case for the Lion this year. Both planned and unplanned journeys should be taking place and where these are purely for business there could be an extra positive twist. This is a time during which you know what you want and have all the energy and determination to get it. New relationships also begin now and even if they begin just as colleagues, they could become stronger over time.

In autumn you may have to stop and retrench a little. You may need to realise that you have gone as far as you can in a particular direction and now you need to start something new. September and October give you the chance to reorder and to be as progressive as you would wish to be. This is one of the best periods of the year for your love life and for making good impressions on almost everyone. Some unexpected travel may become possible towards the end of October.

November and December see some extremely positive trends, especially at home. The Christmas period should be especially enjoyable, with a desire on your part to make it the best celebration you can remember. Avoid family disputes between Christmas and New Year and concentrate on having fun. Let others do at least some of the work.

January

2019

Your Month at a Glance

(+) = Opportunities are around   (−) = Be on the defensive   ● = Life is pretty ordinary

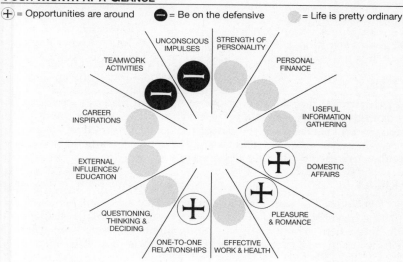

TEAMWORK ACTIVITIES

UNCONSCIOUS IMPULSES

STRENGTH OF PERSONALITY

PERSONAL FINANCE

CAREER INSPIRATIONS

USEFUL INFORMATION GATHERING

EXTERNAL INFLUENCES/ EDUCATION

DOMESTIC AFFAIRS

QUESTIONING, THINKING & DECIDING

PLEASURE & ROMANCE

ONE-TO-ONE RELATIONSHIPS

EFFECTIVE WORK & HEALTH

January Highs and Lows

Here I show you how the rhythms of the Moon will affect you this month. Like the tide, your energies and abilities will rise and fall with its pattern. When it is above the centre line, go for it, when it is below, you should be resting.

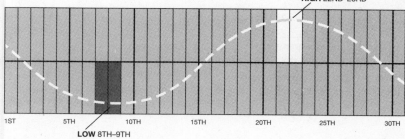

HIGH 22ND–23RD

1ST   5TH   10TH   15TH   20TH   25TH   30TH

LOW 8TH–9TH

45

1 TUESDAY   *Moon Age Day 25   Moon Sign Scorpio*

Some unusual people may attract you this New Year's Day. This is no bad thing, particularly since your own quirky side is also clearly on display. While you are likely to be enjoying the end of the holidays now, you will soon need to get yourself into a positive frame of mind regarding potential changes at work; the faster you do so, the greater headway you will make.

2 WEDNESDAY   *Moon Age Day 26   Moon Sign Scorpio*

A little positive thinking can go a long way at the moment and can bring you to some extremely happy experiences. There is no doubt that you receive a good deal of attention, even from people who have not figured prominently in your life up to now. Advancement could be on the way for some.

3 THURSDAY   *Moon Age Day 27   Moon Sign Sagittarius*

Adopt an attitude that shows everyone around you that you are taking life in your stride and things should go well. What might be more important in the longer-term is that you also manage to convince yourself of this fact. In practical matters you can get ahead simply by applying a little logic to issues that others are having difficulty addressing.

4 FRIDAY   *Moon Age Day 28   Moon Sign Sagittarius*

Don't take yourself or your ideas for granted today. On many occasions you will have a much better idea of the direction your life is taking than anyone in your immediate vicinity. Congratulations might be in order somewhere in your family or friendship circle and it won't hold you up to offer them.

5 SATURDAY   *Moon Age Day 0   Moon Sign Capricorn*

Leave work matters on the back burner for at least one day this weekend. Trends offer plenty of potential for having fun and even family chores can be much more interesting than you may have expected. Conforming to the ideas and opinions of certain family members almost certainly will not be easy, however.

6 SUNDAY   *Moon Age Day 1   Moon Sign Capricorn*

This ought to be a fairly good day in all areas. Practically speaking you have your eye on the ball and won't easily be deterred from a course of action you know you ought to be following. Get some physical exercise if you can. The weather may not be fine but a good, long walk would suit you well.

7 MONDAY
Moon Age Day 2   Moon Sign Capricorn

Self-expression appears to be the key to happiness as this new working week gets underway. Leos who are involved in further education stand a chance of learning something to their advantage, while all Leos should be able to make small financial gains under the prevailing trends.

8 TUESDAY
Moon Age Day 3   Moon Sign Aquarius

With the lunar low coming along today it would be sensible to realise that you can't do everything yourself. Better by far to look towards the expertise of others, some of whom can be of great use to you now. Not the best day of the month for trying to move any mountains, but an ideal time for planning instead.

9 WEDNESDAY
Moon Age Day 4   Moon Sign Aquarius

Although things will probably still be fairly quiet, you can find time to look ahead and to lay down some specific plans. Conforming to the expectations others have of you appears to be easier right now than might have been the case at the start of the year. All in all, the lunar low may end up being a more successful period than you might have imagined.

10 THURSDAY
Moon Age Day 5   Moon Sign Pisces

This is the high point of the month as far as your ego is concerned, though whether this is a strictly positive state of affairs remains to be seen. Try to temper your tendency to push yourself forward with just a little modesty because that will endear you to others. A degree of popularity is important now.

11 FRIDAY
Moon Age Day 6   Moon Sign Pisces

Achieving a state of balance is your goal for today. There is much that craves your attention in a practical sense and that means getting on in a progressive manner. At the same time, there are planetary influences that virtually insist you take a broader view and plan ahead. Leos need to be jugglers today.

12 SATURDAY
Moon Age Day 7   Moon Sign Pisces

You should make room today for getting on side with your partner, or other family members. Don't be in the least surprised if you discover that you have an admirer because this is something that can happen at any stage now. Some of the people who are looking at you favourably come from surprising areas of your life.

13 SUNDAY
Moon Age Day 8   Moon Sign Aries

This is the best time of all for entertaining new ideas. Christmas and the New Year at last recede into the background and for the first time in several weeks you are clearly looking forward. New intellectual interests captivate you and there could be a little more in the way of financial good luck coming your way at any time now.

14 MONDAY
Moon Age Day 9   Moon Sign Aries

Today is the best day of the month so far for going specifically after what you want. Don't be held back by people who appear determined to throw a spanner in the works and make sure that you look and plan ahead carefully. It may be difficult to remain focused on many tasks at once but you are, after all, a child of Leo.

15 TUESDAY
Moon Age Day 10   Moon Sign Taurus

Powerful and sustained relationships are the ones that offer you the most at the present time. Conforming to the expectations of others won't always be easy, especially at work. Get any shopping you have to do out of the way early in the day and perhaps take a break from your responsibilities if you get the chance.

16 WEDNESDAY
Moon Age Day 11   Moon Sign Taurus

Getting out and about should now be very rewarding. You are also in a good position to get what you want, particularly in a romantic sense. The attitude of a friend might puzzle you somewhat but bear in mind that it would be sensible to ask a few leading questions before you react as Leos are inclined to do.

17 THURSDAY
Moon Age Day 12   Moon Sign Taurus

Today finds you in a dynamic mood, particularly with regard to your career. If you are a student, you should find that your studies come easily and virtually all Leos will be registering a very definite improvement in terms of personal popularity. Don't be surprised if someone wants to know you better.

18 FRIDAY
Moon Age Day 13   Moon Sign Gemini

You may have got out of the habit of a particular task or set of jobs that you know to be very important. This Friday offers you the chance to look at them again and to get on side with a person who hasn't been all that easy to deal with of late. You will be amazed at just how much you can get done.

19 SATURDAY

Getting yourself organised is what life is really about today. Strongly confident, you are able to tell the whole world what you want, and how you intend to go about getting it. There may be necessary changes in the pipeline but this is no time to be shying away from any of them.

20 SUNDAY

Your intellectual thought processes are sharp and get better the more you find yourself in open discussion with others. The Leo grit is evident and it is highly unlikely that anyone will get in your way. Something you have been looking forward to might not prove quite as interesting or rewarding as you had hoped.

21 MONDAY

Look around carefully because nobody is better at making the best of opportunities than you are right now. Not everything you want will be forthcoming but when it isn't, unfortunately you may have only yourself to blame. In the best of all worlds, you will usually only have to ask for what you want before it comes your way.

22 TUESDAY

You have an abundance of luck on your side right now and this part of the working week to put the lunar high into positive operation. Although there have clearly been times this month when your progressive tendencies have not been given room to show, today is very different. Simply decide what you want and go for it.

23 WEDNESDAY

Once again this is a day during which you will be pleased to do your own thing, no matter what others think about the situation. There is also time for caring and sharing but in most matters you will actively want to be in the driving seat. Few will argue with a Leo in full flow, which is what you are today.

24 THURSDAY

What you hear right now in connection with your work is well worth mulling over carefully. You don't generally listen too much to gossip but it ought to be worthwhile doing so for the next couple of days. The deeper and more spiritual side of Leo is now on display, which might surprise a few people.

25 FRIDAY
Moon Age Day 20   Moon Sign Virgo

When it comes to any sort of practical task, it appears you have all the help you could possibly need today. Of course, you might have to open your mouth and say what you need, but that shouldn't come at all hard to you. Concentrate on the most important matters early in the day and enjoy yourself later.

26 SATURDAY
Moon Age Day 21   Moon Sign Libra

A rather busy phase at work finds you too stressed to take full advantage of some of the opportunities that the weekend offers. Perhaps you are bringing your work home with you or else thinking about it so much you simply fail to register many of the offers and opportunities that come your way socially.

27 SUNDAY
Moon Age Day 22   Moon Sign Libra

There are gains coming your way, even if you are not particularly looking for them. What should work out well for you at present is listening to the advice of people you really rate. On the other hand, you will be staying right away from individuals you find tedious or tiresome.

28 MONDAY
Moon Age Day 23   Moon Sign Scorpio

Present influences make it very easy for you to do things, which could be something of a curse if others accuse you of being too smart for your own good. All the same, you need to seek your own course, even if this means getting on the wrong side of someone who is really important to you.

29 TUESDAY
Moon Age Day 24   Moon Sign Scorpio

There are rewarding times in store and all you really have to do to make the most of them is to be in the right place at the right time. Intuition helps again, leading to a time that offers a great deal of variety and the chance to make impressions on people who could prove to be important later.

30 WEDNESDAY
Moon Age Day 25   Moon Sign Sagittarius

Don't take all the world's troubles on your own shoulders. You will get ahead far better if you take things steadily and deal with issues that arise one at a time. Romance could be the best place to look for comfort and reassurance, even if you find yourself in the arms of someone rather surprising.

31 THURSDAY

If you take chances today, choose them carefully. Risks are fine, just as long as they are calculated. Leo is sometimes inclined to push matters just for the sake of doing so, though behaving in this manner at the moment won't get you very far at all and might lead to a degree of confusion you could do without.

February

2019

Your Month at a Glance

⊕ = Opportunities are around ⬤ = Be on the defensive ◯ = Life is pretty ordinary

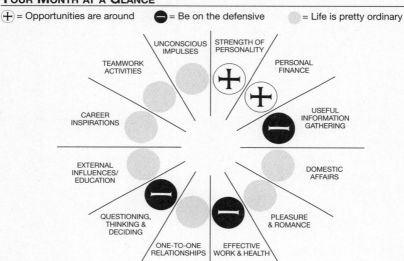

UNCONSCIOUS IMPULSES

STRENGTH OF PERSONALITY

TEAMWORK ACTIVITIES

PERSONAL FINANCE

CAREER INSPIRATIONS

USEFUL INFORMATION GATHERING

EXTERNAL INFLUENCES/ EDUCATION

DOMESTIC AFFAIRS

QUESTIONING, THINKING & DECIDING

PLEASURE & ROMANCE

ONE-TO-ONE RELATIONSHIPS

EFFECTIVE WORK & HEALTH

February Highs and Lows

Here I show you how the rhythms of the Moon will affect you this month. Like the tide, your energies and abilities will rise and fall with its pattern. When it is above the centre line, go for it, when it is below, you should be resting.

HIGH 18TH–19TH

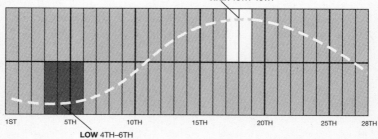

1ST   5TH   10TH   15TH   20TH   25TH   28TH

LOW 4TH–6TH

1 FRIDAY   *Moon Age Day 27   Moon Sign Sagittarius*

Today could be quite sluggish in a professional sense, which is why you are now much more likely to rely on the help and support of those around you. Concentrate on matters that you know to be most important and leave the rest until another day. In your spare moments, you might choose to read.

2 SATURDAY   *Moon Age Day 28   Moon Sign Capricorn*

Today's greatest source of joy and pleasure comes from your association with those around you. This could be at work, or alternatively may come once you are finished with the daily round. Sensitive and caring, you show the warmest side of Leo and will be particularly concerned to support the underdog.

3 SUNDAY   *Moon Age Day 29   Moon Sign Capricorn*

General routines may distract you from ideas you know to be revolutionary and stimulating. Once again it might be necessary to look carefully at what the day requires and to leave alone those jobs that are not essential. Avoid becoming bored at all costs and when assessing others, use your intuition.

4 MONDAY   *Moon Age Day 0   Moon Sign Aquarius*

Enthusiasm is lacking and there isn't anything you can do about it. The lunar low is sapping your strength and resolve, leaving you feeling you have little choice but to go with the flow. Leave important decisions until later and content yourself with what you have at the moment.

5 TUESDAY   *Moon Age Day 1   Moon Sign Aquarius*

This is definitely another day during which you should slow down and take things one at a time. There is absolutely no point in rushing anything because that will be ultimately counter-productive. Allow others to make the running and be willing to let them organise what you should be doing.

6 WEDNESDAY   *Moon Age Day 2   Moon Sign Aquarius*

You should be doing your very best to establish new social contacts this week and today is as good a time as any to get started. When it comes to words of love, you are dredging up more than a romantic poet! This is a little unusual for Leo so you could surprise your partner or someone else dear to your heart.

7 THURSDAY
Moon Age Day 3   Moon Sign Pisces

Maybe you should not try too hard to gain the ear of colleagues or to influence the outcome of specific events today. You are not working at your best and would gain from a short period of limited isolation. You might decide to curl up somewhere with a good book, or better still some sort of puzzle.

8 FRIDAY
Moon Age Day 4   Moon Sign Pisces

You make very entertaining company at present. The fact is that you are outgoing enough to be fun yet showing a really sensitive side that others don't always see and which they really like. Your confidence could be a little lacking, especially when there are important decisions that simply have to be made.

9 SATURDAY
Moon Age Day 5   Moon Sign Aries

A passing astrological trend leaves you somewhat muddle-headed today, so it would be sensible not to make too many decisions if you can possibly avoid doing so. Routines are on your mind, even if you try to shirk them, and it might be better to simply get them out of the way and clear the decks for action.

10 SUNDAY
Moon Age Day 6   Moon Sign Aries

This is definitely the best time to broaden your personal horizons. You can do this by carefully watching what is going on around you. Many of the ideas you have are a great deal better than those of people in your environment. Convincing them that you know best ought to be easy if you remain calm.

11 MONDAY
Moon Age Day 7   Moon Sign Aries

Slowly but surely your practical skills are beginning to show themselves more fully. Step by careful step, you are able to get ahead and to convince those around you that you know what you are doing. In terms of money, now is the time to begin taking the odd chance because calculated risks pay off.

12 TUESDAY
Moon Age Day 8   Moon Sign Taurus

There are serious decisions to be taken at the moment and not all of them are instantly recognisable. Some deep thought is required and you certainly cannot afford to take chances in the way that Leo is sometimes inclined to do. If necessary, seek out the help of someone who is a consummate professional in their own field.

13 WEDNESDAY
Moon Age Day 9   Moon Sign Taurus

Group encounters interest you greatly, though you might have to reorder your schedule somewhat in order to get the best from them. If you don't have time to do everything that seems to be necessary, you could try delegation. This isn't always easy for your zodiac sign but is sometimes necessary.

14 THURSDAY
Moon Age Day 10   Moon Sign Gemini

A little positive thinking can have a great bearing on the way things are going at the moment. With plenty of energy and a great determination to do what you instinctively know is right, push on with your ideas, whilst at the same time listening carefully to what those around you have to say.

15 FRIDAY
Moon Age Day 11   Moon Sign Gemini

You have a lot to say for yourself at the moment but there isn't anything particularly surprising about that. What is slightly different is that you are also so willing to follow the ideas and opinions coming in from outside. This combination of your own common sense and the experience of others should be a winning combination.

16 SATURDAY
Moon Age Day 12   Moon Sign Cancer

Romantically speaking there can be big things happening for Leo at the moment. This can be a weekend of some very important and far-reaching encounters, especially for Lions who are presently without a permanent attachment. Don't turn down the chance of a date just because you are nervous.

17 SUNDAY
Moon Age Day 13   Moon Sign Cancer

Social matters and those involving co-operation with others should go rather well on this Sunday and be enlightening. There are possible small gains to be made to your finances but it still isn't the right time to push the boat out. If you are shopping for a dinner, a party or a reception, don't take the first quote you are offered.

18 MONDAY
Moon Age Day 14   Moon Sign Leo

As trends bring a boost to your personal energies, this week could prove to be the best so far this year. Although the winter weather might prevent you from going far, you will still be in the mood to travel if you can. Leo can be the most intrepid of all the zodiac signs and you prove this at present.

19 TUESDAY
Moon Age Day 15   Moon Sign Leo

A word in the right ear could go a long way to getting you what you want from life. The lunar high presents you with new and better chances to get ahead and you prefer people who are very similar in nature to yourself. There is just the slightest chance that you prove contrary in personal matters.

20 WEDNESDAY
Moon Age Day 16   Moon Sign Virgo

When it comes to promoting your career you could hardly have better trends than the ones that are surrounding you at the moment. Concentrate on the task at hand in practical matters but do be willing to stick your neck out when it comes to telling the world what you feel about specific issues.

21 THURSDAY
Moon Age Day 17   Moon Sign Virgo

You like a hands-on approach and though present trends make that more difficult, you can concentrate on those matters you understand only too well. Avoid family arguments and get the best out of intimate relationships, which look extremely good for the moment. Don't be afraid to admit your limitations, even in public.

22 FRIDAY
Moon Age Day 18   Moon Sign Libra

Certain compromises may be necessary today and if face up to this early, you can avoid a little heartache and soul-searching later. Just do what you know is right and you won't go far wrong. Don't question your own judgement over matters you know you understand.

23 SATURDAY
Moon Age Day 19   Moon Sign Libra

Even those tasks that you have been doing for years can now be undertaken in a new spirit that will make them far more enjoyable. Spend just a little time planning how you want to get things done and find ways to convince yourself that you are performing better and more cheerfully.

24 SUNDAY
Moon Age Day 20   Moon Sign Scorpio

In dealings with the world at large it is now very important to avoid a 'know-it-all' attitude. It won't get you very far and you are dealing with people who are generally intuitive. Avoid politics of any sort at the moment but be as frank and honest you can throughout the whole day.

25 MONDAY
Moon Age Day 21   Moon Sign Scorpio

Don't trust everything you hear today because a fair proportion of it is likely to be wrong. Use a combination of common sense and intuition and you won't go far wrong. When possible, fall back on your previous experience and also be willing to listen to people who are more worldly wise than you might sometimes be.

26 TUESDAY
Moon Age Day 22   Moon Sign Sagittarius

This is a favourable period for important discussions and for coming to terms with a few limitations you were unwilling to recognise earlier. Conversations are good because they offer material to feed your own imagination and you should find yourself to be highly creative as the week moves on.

27 WEDNESDAY
Moon Age Day 23   Moon Sign Sagittarius

You should not be too impulsive when it comes to buying anything today and it might be suggested that big shopping sprees need to be delayed for a while. It doesn't matter how good a bargain looks right now, in a week or two you could do better. Find ways to enjoy yourself that don't cost very much.

28 THURSDAY
Moon Age Day 24   Moon Sign Sagittarius

There is a desire now to get things done as quickly as possible but is this always the best policy? It seems that for the moment it isn't. One job done properly is far better than half a dozen that you have to tackle again later. Be very sure of your footing, especially in issues you are wary of.

March

2019

Your Month at a Glance

$\oplus$ = Opportunities are around $\ominus$ = Be on the defensive   ⬤ = Life is pretty ordinary

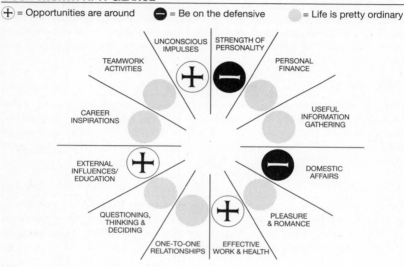

TEAMWORK ACTIVITIES

UNCONSCIOUS IMPULSES

STRENGTH OF PERSONALITY

PERSONAL FINANCE

CAREER INSPIRATIONS

USEFUL INFORMATION GATHERING

EXTERNAL INFLUENCES/ EDUCATION

DOMESTIC AFFAIRS

QUESTIONING, THINKING & DECIDING

ONE-TO-ONE RELATIONSHIPS

EFFECTIVE WORK & HEALTH

PLEASURE & ROMANCE

March Highs and Lows

Here I show you how the rhythms of the Moon will affect you this month. Like the tide, your energies and abilities will rise and fall with its pattern. When it is above the centre line, go for it, when it is below, you should be resting.

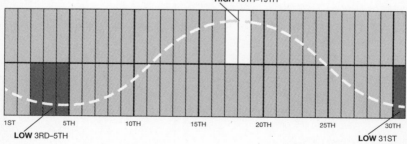

HIGH 18TH–19TH

1ST   5TH   10TH   15TH   20TH   25TH   30TH

LOW 3RD–5TH

LOW 31ST

1 FRIDAY
Moon Age Day 25   Moon Sign Capricorn

A plan of action out there in the competitive world may turn out to be rather less useful that it first appears to be. For this reason, act with circumspection and don't allow your enthusiasm to get the better of you. Avoid confrontation with people who can be of use to you and who are really trying to help.

2 SATURDAY
Moon Age Day 26   Moon Sign Capricorn

You won't be able to remain the centre of attention today but there is a positive side to this state of affairs. If you are not in the limelight, you are far less likely to be criticised, especially for matters that are not really your concern. Refuse to be involved in situations that cannot benefit you in the slightest.

3 SUNDAY
Moon Age Day 27   Moon Sign Aquarius

This is hardly going to be one of the best days of the month for you. The Moon is in your opposite sign and that means you have to tread carefully. Other people may take offence at things you have to say, even though no insult is intended. Close friends are the people to be with, together with family members who know you well.

4 MONDAY
Moon Age Day 28   Moon Sign Aquarius

Although life may not be sparkling at this time you can be sure that things will get better as the day wears on. Give and take will help a lot, together with at least some time spent on your own. Your confidence begins to increase after lunch and by the evening you could find yourself in the right mood to socialise.

5 TUESDAY
Moon Age Day 29   Moon Sign Aquarius

This is a wonderful time for social get togethers and for showing a friendly face to the world in general. Now you enjoy a higher personal profile and should not be shy about putting your ideas forward. A slightly negative phase for Leo should have come to an end and your more forceful traits back in evidence.

6 WEDNESDAY ☿
Moon Age Day 0   Moon Sign Pisces

A more frugal approach to money matters may be both advisable and even necessary. It's really just a case of thinking before you spend lavishly on anything. Keep up your efforts to get ahead at work and don't be afraid to seek the support of people who are in the best position to lend you a helping hand.

7 THURSDAY   ☿   *Moon Age Day 1   Moon Sign Pisces*

Some good news could be coming in from a number of different directions. This is a period during which you may be getting positive mail and a longed-for ambition could be realised before long. It is also possible that you receive a helping hand from a quite unexpected direction before today is over.

8 FRIDAY   ☿   *Moon Age Day 2   Moon Sign Aries*

Whatever is happening around you now, it is clear that you want to be a part of it. Although there are things going on that demand your attention, you will also be expected to fulfil specific expectations in a family sense. Avoid getting involved in any sort of scheme that you know instinctively might be somewhat shady.

9 SATURDAY   ☿   *Moon Age Day 3   Moon Sign Aries*

If you try to do everything at once you will find that something has to give. Try to pace yourself a little and leave some jobs for others. There are plenty of people around at the moment who would be only too willing to lend a hand and you should be humble enough to allow them their moment of glory too.

10 SUNDAY   ☿   *Moon Age Day 4   Moon Sign Taurus*

Everyday discussions have plenty of cut and thrust. You are saying what you think, which is fine as long as you remember that some people are quite sensitive by nature and may not respond well to what you have on your mind. It's important to balance telling the truth as you see it with avoiding the possibility of giving offence.

11 MONDAY   ☿   *Moon Age Day 5   Moon Sign Taurus*

Today is a career day and a time when you will be addressing the need to push ahead and perhaps to gain advancements of some sort. Look out for superiors who are clearly in a position to do you a lot of good and who are simply waiting for you to ask. In any practical situation, confidence is now the key to success.

12 TUESDAY   ☿   *Moon Age Day 6   Moon Sign Taurus*

There is a possibility that you will find yourself at odds with others regarding issues that really don't demand too much attention. If you know you are nit-picking, then it is also clear that you can stop. There are advantages to be gained today, simply from being in the right place at the right time.

13 WEDNESDAY ☿ *Moon Age Day 7   Moon Sign Gemini*

Strong-willed and determined, there is just a chance these tendencies will get you into some trouble at this time. No matter how much you think you are correct regarding specific issues, there are always other points of view. It is extremely important at the moment that you stop, look and listen. Information coming from strange directions can be of great assistance.

14 THURSDAY ☿ *Moon Age Day 8   Moon Sign Gemini*

Whenever action is the key to success, you are there, champing at the bit. Once again the advice is to move forward carefully and not to overload your nervous system. Problems are there to the solved and that is what you will do. Be selective, however, as some issues probably are not even worth your attention.

15 FRIDAY ☿ *Moon Age Day 9   Moon Sign Cancer*

If it comes to a battle of wills today, it is quite possible that you will choose to withdraw. This is extremely unusual behaviour for the Lion but the fact is that you are feeling extremely confident at the moment. Part of this mind-set tells you that you don't have anything to prove and that you do not always have to win at any cost.

16 SATURDAY ☿ *Moon Age Day 10   Moon Sign Cancer*

A social contact might let you down, though long-term friends are much less likely to cause you problems. You need to choose your contacts very carefully at the moment and should not allow sentiment to get in the way of decisions you know to by very important.

17 SUNDAY ☿ *Moon Age Day 11   Moon Sign Cancer*

Today is likely to be both busy and interesting. If you have to do things that go against the grain, you should discover that even this offers a degree of interest you didn't expect. Contributing to the success of others is something that ought to appeal, especially since this is a typical Leo trait.

18 MONDAY ☿ *Moon Age Day 12   Moon Sign Leo*

Along comes the physical and mental peak that you have been looking for all month. In addition to the lunar high the Sun is now in a really good position, which is bound to bring support and a very cheerful attitude. There is plenty to be done but the reserves of energy you have at present are deep and enduring.

19 TUESDAY   ☿   *Moon Age Day 13   Moon Sign Leo*

A word in the right ear could see you shifting a host of obstacles today and getting on with things at a good pace. Although not everyone will be on your side at the moment, in the main there is plenty of help when you need it the most. Your attitude is positive and you seem to have a particular penchant for enjoying yourself.

20 WEDNESDAY ☿   *Moon Age Day 14   Moon Sign Virgo*

A period of your life comes along in which you may be feeling somewhat negative, particularly about romantic attachments. The truth is that you need a degree of change, perhaps because you are feeling somehow isolated. Digging up old contacts from the past might appeal, though you are generally restless right now.

21 THURSDAY   ☿   *Moon Age Day 15   Moon Sign Virgo*

You can now put some of your versatility to use, particularly at work. When you are away from the professional arena, you should notice that personal attachments seem somehow more rewarding and offer you incentives to be as kind as you can be to someone who really counts in your life.

22 FRIDAY   ☿   *Moon Age Day 16   Moon Sign Libra*

Although you are still generally interested in life, events in and around your home prove less than inspiring. Maybe you need a break and to be in the company of people who get your juices flowing. Set yourself some sort of challenge; that's a strategy that generally works if Leo is becoming bored.

23 SATURDAY   ☿   *Moon Age Day 17   Moon Sign Libra*

You can now be the star attraction in a social sense, at the beginning of a weekend that has a great deal to offer you. You should also be willing to put extra effort is put into those jobs you really favour, maybe at the expense of tasks you don't want to do. This is a recurring theme during March and should be guarded against.

24 SUNDAY   ☿   *Moon Age Day 18   Moon Sign Scorpio*

Though you are now clearly enjoying the mental challenges that life has to offer, there are times when it will be difficult to fit in everything you really want to do. The secret is to plan ahead and to take on those social demands that interest you the most. It is the undertones of what loved ones are saying that you notice the most.

25 MONDAY ☿ *Moon Age Day 19 Moon Sign Scorpio*

A lift to your love life comes along as the weekend disappears into the background. Any negatives are left behind and all incentives now look crisper and sharper than has been the case of late. With a degree of excitement you can't really explain, there are significant gains to be made around every corner.

26 TUESDAY ☿ *Moon Age Day 20 Moon Sign Sagittarius*

You should be able to keep up a varied and highly stimulating love life right now. Typical of you, there are not enough hours in a day to fit in everything you would wish to do but if you are selective you should discover possibilities that had not occurred to you before. Your finances may strengthen around now.

27 WEDNESDAY ☿ *Moon Age Day 21 Moon Sign Sagittarius*

Not only are you presently feeling a good deal less assertive than has been the case, your general sensitivity is going right off the scale. The spiritual heart of Leo is diametrically opposed to the go-getter you sometimes have to be. Use today to explore the deep, inner quality that you so rarely address.

28 THURSDAY ☿ *Moon Age Day 22 Moon Sign Capricorn*

Your co-operative spirit is strong, a fact that isn't lost on others, many of whom are quite happy to pitch in with you. There is a distinct possibility that you can come to terms with someone who has openly disliked you in the past. Getting rid of an enemy may prove far more important than you presently appreciate.

29 FRIDAY *Moon Age Day 23 Moon Sign Capricorn*

The more ambitious you choose to be today, the better things are likely to go for you. There are moments today when you feel as though you could rule the world, though of course this is illusion, so a degree of realism is also called for. Socially speaking, you can make some good starts.

30 SATURDAY *Moon Age Day 24 Moon Sign Capricorn*

Recent ideas and initiatives come back into your mind, perhaps because Saturday offers you a chance to look at things in greater detail. Try not to count every tedious step in a job you simply do not want to do. Good times are in store, though for the moment you might be forgiven for missing this fact.

31 SUNDAY

Moon Age Day 25   Moon Sign Aquarius

Keep your sights low today and don't expect great achievements. This is not to suggest that you give up altogether. The lunar low this month is a short affair because there are planetary positions that swamp its influence. The most you are likely to experience today is some small frustrations and a few niggling doubts.

2019

YOUR MONTH AT A GLANCE

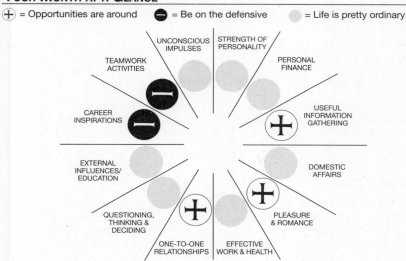

⊕ = Opportunities are around   ⊖ = Be on the defensive   ● = Life is pretty ordinary

- UNCONSCIOUS IMPULSES
- STRENGTH OF PERSONALITY
- TEAMWORK ACTIVITIES
- PERSONAL FINANCE
- CAREER INSPIRATIONS
- USEFUL INFORMATION GATHERING
- EXTERNAL INFLUENCES/ EDUCATION
- DOMESTIC AFFAIRS
- QUESTIONING, THINKING & DECIDING
- PLEASURE & ROMANCE
- ONE-TO-ONE RELATIONSHIPS
- EFFECTIVE WORK & HEALTH

APRIL HIGHS AND LOWS

Here I show you how the rhythms of the Moon will affect you this month. Like the tide, your energies and abilities will rise and fall with its pattern. When it is above the centre line, go for it, when it is below, you should be resting.

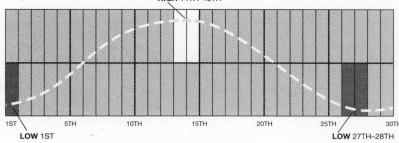

HIGH 14TH–15TH

1ST   5TH   10TH   15TH   20TH   25TH   30TH

LOW 1ST

LOW 27TH–28TH

1 MONDAY
Moon Age Day 26   Moon Sign Aquarius

A new month dawns and you are in such a good frame of mind that you won't care at all if people play the odd April fool joke on you. Leo can be humorous and even silly on occasions, a fact that is in evidence now. People like you, and it's a great feeling to know that you are number one in someone's chart.

2 TUESDAY
Moon Age Day 27   Moon Sign Pisces

If you want a day during which it is possible to get your own way most of the time, this is it. You should remember not to be selfish though because it would be all too easy to make an enemy if you push forward with all those Leo guns blazing. Your general attitude is good, especially in personal attachments.

3 WEDNESDAY
Moon Age Day 28   Moon Sign Pisces

A focus on far-reaching matters and less on personal ones should make long journeys and mind-broadening experiences the order of the day. If so, go for it because you have very little to lose. Monetary situations could be rather confused but you will usually reach your objectives in the end, if somewhat messily.

4 THURSDAY
Moon Age Day 29   Moon Sign Pisces

Short-term plans and career ambitions are looking at their best right now and you should certainly do what you can right now to get ahead. Perhaps you have been thinking in terms of advancement or even a change of job? Look around and listen carefully to what is being said, as well as scanning notice boards and newspapers.

5 FRIDAY
Moon Age Day 0   Moon Sign Aries

You are at your best intellectually and will be coming up with some amazing ideas. Use these positive trends to your best advantage and don't allow yourself to be restricted by narrow-minded or bigoted types. You know what you want from life today and the planets are able to help you get it.

6 SATURDAY
Moon Age Day 1   Moon Sign Aries

The weekend arrives again and you can make a great deal of progress in the world as a whole. However, this is certainly not a good time to get on the wrong side of anyone and you would be well advised to treat almost everyone you meet as a potential ally. There are some very strange attachments in the offing.

7 SUNDAY
Moon Age Day 2   Moon Sign Taurus

Your social life ought to get slightly more interesting around now and there are opportunities to pep up your love life too. Don't be surprised if you are encouraged to mix business with pleasure, especially if you are not attached in a romantic sense. Someone is likely to be looking at you very favourably.

8 MONDAY
Moon Age Day 3   Moon Sign Taurus

You have to make room for the emotions of other people today because they are pressing in on your world whether you like it or not. Don't expect total harmony, especially at home. Not everyone is on the same wavelength as you are and some deep understanding seems to be very necessary now.

9 TUESDAY
Moon Age Day 4   Moon Sign Gemini

Look out for a very good day for entertaining at home. On the one hand you are very sociable at the moment but on the other you need to feel the security of your own four walls. You can take care of both situations by inviting people round, for dinner perhaps? Relationship trends are really good.

10 WEDNESDAY
Moon Age Day 5   Moon Sign Gemini

This is likely to be a fruitful and productive time but it does partly depend on your own attitude and that of your closest allies. You tend to stick around people who are naturally positive at the moment and won't want to be associated with those who dither. Take care that you are not accused of bullying tactics.

11 THURSDAY
Moon Age Day 6   Moon Sign Gemini

You tend to be quite a dominant force now and will be more than willing to take command in the workplace. In social situations you are more likely to allow others their head. Your confidence in yourself is very high and when this is the case you discover that you really have very little to prove.

12 FRIDAY
Moon Age Day 7   Moon Sign Cancer

Try to engage in projects that need to be properly finished before you get started with new ones. The fact of the matter is that you are probably biting off more than you can chew and that isn't to be recommended. You may be well ahead in tasks you enjoy but quite far behind on tiresome chores.

13 SATURDAY
Moon Age Day 8   Moon Sign Cancer

Certain relationships and associations might seem to be more trouble than they are worth right now but you need to keep plugging away, even against the odds. Someone you don't see too often is returning to your social scene but you may not be any keener on them now than you were in the past.

14 SUNDAY
Moon Age Day 9   Moon Sign Leo

The lunar high brings a positive response to almost all situations and backs up the excellent planetary trends that exist around you generally. Your powers of communication have rarely been better and it isn't hard for you to get what you want, either in a practical or a romantic sense.

15 MONDAY
Moon Age Day 10   Moon Sign Leo

This is where you put your general good luck to the test. The more you push it, the greater are the potential rewards but it does sometimes take courage of the Leo sort. Don't be in the least surprised if people are gathering round constantly to ask your advice. Simply take this situation in your stride.

16 TUESDAY
Moon Age Day 11   Moon Sign Virgo

When it comes to major initiatives you won't be holding back. This is one of those days when Leo shows its real mettle and insists on getting its own way at every turn. As long as you bear in mind that other people have opinions too, you should be able to get away with pushing your ideas through.

17 WEDNESDAY
Moon Age Day 12   Moon Sign Virgo

Getting along with others today may not be the easiest of tasks. It is likely that those around you seem to be doing everything they can to throw a spanner in the works. Of course, this is just your perception, and you must be wise enough to realise this fact. If you don't, trouble could follow.

18 THURSDAY
Moon Age Day 13   Moon Sign Libra

When it comes to being number one in the social diaries of everyone else, you should have little trouble at present. Make life easy for yourself by showing the real charm of which you are capable. With the year advancing and slightly warmer days on the cards, you should be getting out and about more – if possible do this with friends.

19 FRIDAY
Moon Age Day 14   Moon Sign Libra

Ring the changes as much as possible today. You don't need to tell everyone your business, and indeed it might be a mistake to do so. Continue your past efforts to get ahead in the financial stakes and do be prepared to count every penny right now because you are going to need more cash before very long.

20 SATURDAY
Moon Age Day 15   Moon Sign Scorpio

If you are at loggerheads in a friendship it really would be sensible to stand back and look at things in a different way, rather than slogging it out with someone you actually like very much. To retreat from such a situation is not a sign of defeat, but rather a mark of your intelligence.

21 SUNDAY
Moon Age Day 16   Moon Sign Scorpio

An issue from the past is inclined to raise its head again, much to your disapproval. Treat such situations with circumspection and don't allow yourself to be too quick to react. Patience is a virtue, though all too often it is one you don't possess in great measure. Your confidence might seem lacking, but it is there if you look for it.

22 MONDAY
Moon Age Day 17   Moon Sign Sagittarius

Compromises may be easy at home or in personal attachments, but they are much more difficult at work. There is a great difference between the various sides of your nature right now and this is a situation you really do have to address. Complete one job before you get started on another.

23 TUESDAY
Moon Age Day 18   Moon Sign Sagittarius

Financially and in terms of work, there are now matters that you can simply sit back and allow to mature in their own good time. This allows you moments to look around. Since you are now in a contemplative frame of mind, this is going to prove a rewarding period. All Leos need to sit and think from time to time.

24 WEDNESDAY
Moon Age Day 19   Moon Sign Capricorn

As is often the case you thrust yourself into the very centre of whatever action is taking place in your vicinity. Conforming to the expectations of others will not be all that easy because you so often think they don't know what they are talking about. Balance is hard to find but important if you really want to achieve anything.

25 THURSDAY
Moon Age Day 20   Moon Sign Capricorn

Watch out for financial fluctuations, which might take you more or less by surprise. Your creative potential is good, though may not extend to money matters. In a family sense, you are probably wise enough to let someone else make the running, at least for the next couple of days and maybe even longer.

26 FRIDAY
Moon Age Day 21   Moon Sign Capricorn

It could seem now that personal freedom is the key to contentment and indeed, up to a point, this is true. However, there are other issues that need to be addressed, not least of all the fact that your partner is behaving rather oddly. Instead of simply wondering what it going on, it might be sensible to ask a few leading questions.

27 SATURDAY
Moon Age Day 22   Moon Sign Aquarius

It would probably be best to let others make some of the decisions today. The lunar low is sapping your strength somewhat and making it difficult for you to see the wood for the trees. Just about the only aspect of life that this doesn't bear down on is romance. This is exactly the right day to be whispering words of love.

28 SUNDAY
Moon Age Day 23   Moon Sign Aquarius

Your confidence still isn't exactly high, though if you are willing to listen to your relatives and friends, this doesn't really matter. When it comes to getting things done, it is inevitable that you will constantly be broken off today. That's simply part of the astrological package on offer and there is little or nothing to be done about it.

29 MONDAY
Moon Age Day 24   Moon Sign Pisces

All the practical skills at your disposal are showing themselves clearly as April draws to towards its close. This is probably just as well because so many demands are being made of you. Splitting your responsibilities could be sensible and even sharing a few of them with other people if you can.

30 TUESDAY
Moon Age Day 25   Moon Sign Pisces

Although your social life might seem somewhat less impressive today than you would wish, the situation is within your own hands. Don't be too quick to judge others, especially in personal matters. Simply go with the flow and allow yourself to laugh at the foolishness you observe out there in the wider world.

May

2019

YOUR MONTH AT A GLANCE

⊕ = Opportunities are around   ⊖ = Be on the defensive   ⬤ = Life is pretty ordinary

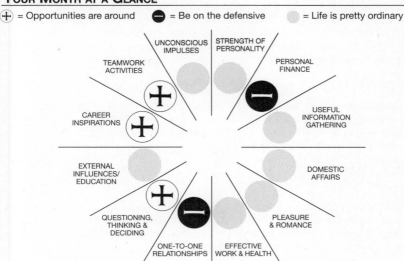

UNCONSCIOUS IMPULSES

STRENGTH OF PERSONALITY

TEAMWORK ACTIVITIES

PERSONAL FINANCE

CAREER INSPIRATIONS

USEFUL INFORMATION GATHERING

EXTERNAL INFLUENCES/ EDUCATION

DOMESTIC AFFAIRS

QUESTIONING, THINKING & DECIDING

PLEASURE & ROMANCE

ONE-TO-ONE RELATIONSHIPS

EFFECTIVE WORK & HEALTH

MAY HIGHS AND LOWS

Here I show you how the rhythms of the Moon will affect you this month. Like the tide, your energies and abilities will rise and fall with its pattern. When it is above the centre line, go for it, when it is below, you should be resting.

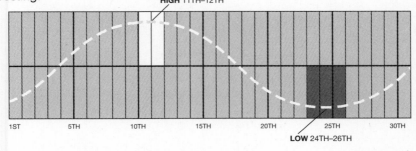

HIGH 11TH–12TH

1ST   5TH   10TH   15TH   20TH   25TH   30TH

LOW 24TH–26TH

1 WEDNESDAY *Moon Age Day 26   Moon Sign Pisces*

Getting along with others certainly does not have to be a battle today, but you tend to see it as such on a few occasions. Listen carefully to what is being said to you, keeping your own opinions on hold until you have done so. In the end you may well realise that your opinions are broadly the same as those of other people.

2 THURSDAY *Moon Age Day 27   Moon Sign Aries*

Happiness to you at the moment is likely to mean being on the move. An early holiday would suit you just fine but if this isn't possible, try to vary your routines as much as possible. Avoid staying in the same place for too long and make sure that variety also represents a strong element of your social life.

3 FRIDAY *Moon Age Day 28   Moon Sign Aries*

Friendships and group encounters take on a particularly pleasant feel right now. You should be feeling confident and that makes the difference between a happy and a miserable Leo. Your creative mood might lead you to think about changes regarding your home.

4 SATURDAY *Moon Age Day 0   Moon Sign Taurus*

There is important news coming your way now, and though you may not be in the best position to take advantage of it, this is a period when it would be quite sensible to keep your ears open. By tomorrow, you will be champing at the bit and anxious to get on. Just for today you tend to be more in planning mode.

5 SUNDAY *Moon Age Day 1   Moon Sign Taurus*

What a wonderful time this would be for getting on the right side of your boss, so it is a shame that many Leos will not be at work today. Nevertheless, you can influence others positively, even in your social and family life. Everything comes together to make you charming, yet incisive and determined.

6 MONDAY *Moon Age Day 2   Moon Sign Taurus*

Financial matters should be looking stronger as the day goes on. Although you may be in a position for a little cautious speculation, some circumspection will definitely be necessary. New ideas could come to you and you will probably be willing to listen to the advice of good friends. Socially speaking you will want to be active.

7 TUESDAY
Moon Age Day 3   Moon Sign Gemini

Some information you receive today could turn out to be very valuable. There are enlightening times ahead and maybe a meeting with people who are going to be of great value in your life eventually. Existing pals want to spend time with you, but there are choices to be made at a time when you are so busy.

8 WEDNESDAY
Moon Age Day 4   Moon Sign Gemini

There is information coming your way at any time now that should prove to be extremely useful. On the personal front, relationships are looking especially good and there could not be a better time than this for speaking words of love to someone who is extra special. The kinder and gentler side of your nature comes to the forefront.

9 THURSDAY
Moon Age Day 5   Moon Sign Cancer

It takes a good deal of courage to admit that you might have been wrong. If you have to eat a little humble pie at some stage today, make sure you do so with a good heart. It would be better to say nothing, rather than to grudgingly concede defeat. Those who know you well have some words of wisdom later.

10 FRIDAY
Moon Age Day 6   Moon Sign Cancer

There is no doubt that you display considerable charm right now. Almost anyone you come across will be noticing it and that means a boost to your personal popularity. Look after money carefully, particularly later in the day, when you may be faced with a bargain that looks just too good. Be wary.

11 SATURDAY
Moon Age Day 7   Moon Sign Leo

Today brings positive aspects to bear on you. With plenty of energy and a great desire to get on, the amount you actually get through can be breathtaking. Avoid family arguments and stay out there in the mainstream of life. That is where you will feel most comfortable and the place you make the greatest impression.

12 SUNDAY
Moon Age Day 8   Moon Sign Leo

Sunday shows a continuation of the generally favourable trends that surround you at present. Although there is plenty to be done, you approach all jobs with a cheerful attitude. If there is a need in your life at the moment to actively tell others how they should behave, this might be a good day to speak out.

13 MONDAY
Moon Age Day 9   Moon Sign Virgo

Information can come from almost any direction at the moment so it would be wise to pay great attention. There could be some shifting and changing necessary in and around your home. For those Leos who are not as young as they once were, help is on hand if you are willing to accept it.

14 TUESDAY
Moon Age Day 10   Moon Sign Virgo

Spirits might not be quite as high as you would wish but that doesn't mean you are particularly slowing down. It may be that you simply don't have quite your usual level of self-confidence, though this situation will change soon enough. By the evening, you will probably be in the mood to party.

15 WEDNESDAY
Moon Age Day 11   Moon Sign Libra

Input and information relating to present schemes and plans are important to you this Wednesday. It does no harm to dream, especially about things that stand a good chance of becoming a reality in the fullness of time. A practical approach to personal situations finds you breaking new ground and explaining yourself wonderfully.

16 THURSDAY
Moon Age Day 12   Moon Sign Libra

Personal money matters should continue to go through a generally settled phase, leaving you with the time to think about other things. Before you do it is worth considering that investments laid down carefully at this time are likely to bring significant dividends later.

17 FRIDAY
Moon Age Day 13   Moon Sign Scorpio

Although there is slightly less in the way of rewards coming from one or two friendships, there are still people around who prove to be reliable. Your concern for family members is probably understandable but not quite as necessary as it appears. Don't be too quick to jump to any conclusion at the moment.

18 SATURDAY
Moon Age Day 14   Moon Sign Scorpio

You have a particularly persuasive tongue at present, so bringing others round to your point of view is extremely easy. No person is better than any other when it comes to getting the assistance you need with a new project, if only because you have the ability to enlist whatever support you need.

19 SUNDAY
Moon Age Day 15   Moon Sign Scorpio

A variety of interests should prove rewarding today and you are much less likely to be nervy or on edge. Leo tends to get a little ragged in a mental sense when it is necessary to concentrate on one fact exclusively. Conforming to social expectations could be something of a chore but is probably necessary.

20 MONDAY
Moon Age Day 16   Moon Sign Sagittarius

A good percentage of your time today is doubtless taken up thinking about practical matters and especially money. Don't push yourself harder than is necessary because social trends are also good and it might be pleasant to spend at least a few hours today simply finding ways to enjoy yourself.

21 TUESDAY
Moon Age Day 17   Moon Sign Sagittarius

There is just a slight accent on the negative now, even if this is not coming specifically from your direction. You can see fewer opportunities on the horizon, a state of affairs that won't please you too much. One thing is certain; arguing for your limitations is going to make them much more obvious to everyone.

22 WEDNESDAY
Moon Age Day 18   Moon Sign Capricorn

A calmer, and even a more contemplative, Lion is now on display. The depth of your thinking is much greater than would usually be the case and you may even surprise yourself with your sensitivity. It's almost as if you can feel the way others are thinking and you can predict their likely actions and responses.

23 THURSDAY
Moon Age Day 19   Moon Sign Capricorn

A friend could probably see much more clearly than you just how a specific investment in terms of money or time could prove to be extremely useful. Because their insights are stronger than yours now, it would be well worthwhile lending them an ear. Confronting opponents is not something you should do today.

24 FRIDAY
Moon Age Day 20   Moon Sign Aquarius

This probably will not be the most dynamic period you have ever lived through, though you actively choose the peace and quiet and it is not imposed on you. Spend time with those you love, together with interesting people who are coming into your life for the first time. Physical activity won't be at a peak.

25 SATURDAY
Moon Age Day 21   Moon Sign Aquarius

Ordinary progress is possible today but anything beyond that is bound to be rather difficult. Once the lunar low is out of the way you can move forward progressively. In the meantime you will have to make do with second best. Remain social and spend as much time as possible with relatives and good friends.

26 SUNDAY
Moon Age Day 22   Moon Sign Aquarius

This is another day on which you are likely to discover that getting ahead is far less easy than would usually be the case. However, today is especially good for planning ahead and for talking to friends and family members alike. Concern for the underdog is also evident – a general trait for Leo.

27 MONDAY
Moon Age Day 23   Moon Sign Pisces

Communication issues are highlighted today, both for positive and negative reasons. Certainly your curiosity is aroused very easily and you may even find yourself chasing a rainbow or two. This is not a day on which to confront others or during which you should take yourself at all seriously.

28 TUESDAY
Moon Age Day 24   Moon Sign Pisces

Emotional matters are apt to preoccupy you now, which is why you need other matters on which to concentrate from time to time. Don't worry too much about the way those around you are behaving. Just as surely as your astrological fortunes fluctuate, so do theirs. Keep an open mind about inevitable changes at home.

29 WEDNESDAY
Moon Age Day 25   Moon Sign Aries

You enjoy being in the social mainstream today and so will probably not be concentrating quite as much on practical matters as has been the case earlier in the month. With the weather improving and late spring blooming around every corner, it becomes more important to you to get out and about.

30 THURSDAY
Moon Age Day 26   Moon Sign Aries

A useful boost to communication skills makes it possible for you to take the plans you have laid down for the upcoming weekend and to modify them positively. Frustration is kept to a minimum though some trends indicate the presence of family members who refuse to conform to your expectations of them.

31 FRIDAY
Moon Age Day 27   Moon Sign Aries

It is not a good idea to believe everything you hear today. Although it is unlikely that anyone is deliberately trying to dupe you, you are more easily fooled at the moment than would generally be the case. Protect your interests in some way, even if you have to go to some trouble to do so.

June
2019

YOUR MONTH AT A GLANCE

⊕ = Opportunities are around   ⊖ = Be on the defensive   ⚫ = Life is pretty ordinary

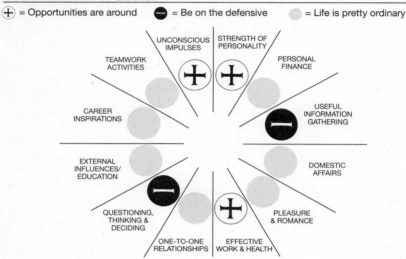

UNCONSCIOUS IMPULSES

STRENGTH OF PERSONALITY

TEAMWORK ACTIVITIES

PERSONAL FINANCE

CAREER INSPIRATIONS

USEFUL INFORMATION GATHERING

EXTERNAL INFLUENCES/ EDUCATION

DOMESTIC AFFAIRS

QUESTIONING, THINKING & DECIDING

PLEASURE & ROMANCE

ONE-TO-ONE RELATIONSHIPS

EFFECTIVE WORK & HEALTH

JUNE HIGHS AND LOWS

Here I show you how the rhythms of the Moon will affect you this month. Like the tide, your energies and abilities will rise and fall with its pattern. When it is above the centre line, go for it, when it is below, you should be resting.

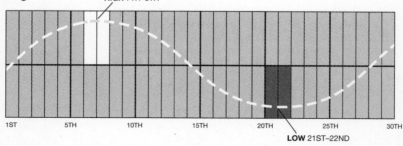

HIGH 7TH–8TH

1ST   5TH   10TH   15TH   20TH   25TH   30TH

LOW 21ST–22ND

78

1 SATURDAY
Moon Age Day 28 · Moon Sign Taurus

Domestically speaking this is a very demanding period. Although there is plenty to keep you busy at work, people at home are definitely seeking your attention. Try to split your time as best you can but avoid crowding your schedule. If necessary, leave practical matters until later.

2 SUNDAY
Moon Age Day 29 Moon Sign Taurus

A genuine love of life ought to be enhanced at the moment as a result of gatherings and meetings with some fairly influential people. You may have to do some serious thinking today but this is hardly likely to have any bearing at all on the personal or social aspects of life. Leave one or two major jobs until tomorrow.

3 MONDAY
Moon Age Day 0 Moon Sign Gemini

Prepare for a practical setback. If this has anything to do with house and home, it could be better to leave others to sort things out. Treat yourself in some way today, by getting out of the house, perhaps with a journey. You still need change and diversity, together with a good social life.

4 TUESDAY
Moon Age Day 1 Moon Sign Gemini

It is possible that there will be some niggles at home, doubtless caused by people who have agendas that are not the same as your own. Avoid tension by refusing to get involved in disputes that are not of your own making. Indeed, you could find yourself negotiating between people who cannot seem to see eye to eye.

5 WEDNESDAY
Moon Age Day 2 Moon Sign Cancer

You are very curious at the moment and will be investigating all sorts of matters that are finding their way to your door. Leaving no stone unturned, you keep your ears and eyes open, whilst asking exactly the right questions. Love is also a priority today, with attention coming your way before the day is out.

6 THURSDAY
Moon Age Day 3 Moon Sign Cancer

It is possible you will discover today that over-optimism could be something of a drawback. Be circumspect, but take care not to come across as too suspicious. With the warmer summer weather now beginning to show itself, you may be keen to get out and about, maybe even planning a holiday before long.

7 FRIDAY
Moon Age Day 4   Moon Sign Leo

To add icing to what is already a fairly good cake, along comes the lunar high. You will be positive in your actions and inspirational in your ideas. Keep your touch light and social, and mix with as many different types of people as you can. If you have been considering quite significant changes at work, this could be the time to implement them.

8 SATURDAY
Moon Age Day 5   Moon Sign Leo

During this period you are able to steam ahead, even if the fact that it is a weekend slows your professional aspirations somewhat. A good day for shopping and for acquiring something you have been wanting for a while. Although there is a lot of work ahead of you, the prospects are looking especially good.

9 SUNDAY
Moon Age Day 6   Moon Sign Virgo

Positive thinking can have a tremendous bearing on your success today. Of course you will have to put in some effort too but there is little doubt that if you believe in yourself, benefits will come along. Avoid pointless routines. These will just bore you and fail to bring any real gain. Friends should be helpful.

10 MONDAY
Moon Age Day 7   Moon Sign Virgo

Just at the moment a plan of action that you were going to work on today might be better put on hold. This is a potentially quieter day and one during which good luck is not quite so inclined to be on your side. As far as your home is concerned, this is likely to be the place where you feel most comfortable for now.

11 TUESDAY
Moon Age Day 8   Moon Sign Virgo

Nobody is going to talk you out of anything you really want to do. The stubborn side of Leo is on display and it makes you much less likely to be nudged in any direction that goes against the grain. Don't take this tendency too far, particularly when you know for certain that people have your best interests at heart.

12 WEDNESDAY
Moon Age Day 9   Moon Sign Libra

If there is anything irritating you today it would be best to get it out in the open as soon as possible. A change of attitude might be necessary in order for you to get the best out of the day and there might also be confidences to keep in personal attachments. Find time at some stage to enjoy the warmer summer weather.

13 THURSDAY
Moon Age Day 10   Moon Sign Libra

People around you are in a good position to strengthen your sense of comfort and security at home. This is probably not a time when you will be trying to achieve too much in a practical sense, mainly because you are too busy looking relationships and the very important part they play in your life.

14 FRIDAY
Moon Age Day 11   Moon Sign Scorpio

This would be an especially good time for group encounters, so sticking to just one individual doesn't suit you particularly well right now. There could be a conflict here because someone who is especially close to you needs constant reassurance now. Walking this tightrope isn't easy, but it can be achieved with concentration.

15 SATURDAY
Moon Age Day 12   Moon Sign Scorpio

Initiating new ideas can be very productive now, both for medium and long-term objectives. Share some of your schemes with people who are in the know and avoid keeping things to yourself that depend on co-operation. An over suspicious attitude right now will only hold you back later.

16 SUNDAY
Moon Age Day 13   Moon Sign Sagittarius

Don't allow domestic obligations to get in the way of matters that are likely to be enjoyable and possibly also rewarding. It might seem at times as though you have nothing particularly interesting to say, though those around you would be surprised at this because they find you fascinating.

17 MONDAY
Moon Age Day 14   Moon Sign Sagittarius

Romantic involvements may not be offering quite the potential they did a couple of days ago. The fault is not yours but comes from a combination of astrological trends, few of which are favouring this aspect of life. On a practical front things should be better and you might choose today to seek advancement.

18 TUESDAY
Moon Age Day 15   Moon Sign Capricorn

Avoid getting obsessed about anything, particularly a work issue that you cannot alter. If you are willing to go with the flow and to co-operate with people you instinctively trust, matters are apt to sort themselves out. This leaves you somewhat freer to get on with patching up a dent in an important relationship.

19 WEDNESDAY
Moon Age Day 16   Moon Sign Capricorn

You are now in a generally competitive frame of mind and able to take the world on. What might prove somewhat frustrating on this particular day is the realisation that nobody wants to confront you. All is peace and harmony in your vicinity and it would certainly be a shame to change that, simply because you are restless.

20 THURSDAY
Moon Age Day 17   Moon Sign Capricorn

The chances are that you have some reason to celebrate today, which you will do with great willingness. A change of scene or a social get-together really suits you right now. Some Leos may even be considering taking a long break at this time. If so, you could hardly have chosen more wisely because trends are very favourable.

21 FRIDAY
Moon Age Day 18   Moon Sign Aquarius

Not everything is going to go entirely as you would wish during the period of the lunar low. For today and tomorrow it is best to remember that planning, as opposed to doing, is the best key to ultimate gains. Socially speaking it is likely you will stick with the people who have been in your life for some time.

22 SATURDAY
Moon Age Day 19   Moon Sign Aquarius

Don't be too concerned with the future, except in terms of looking ahead in your mind and sorting out minor details. Expect a quiet start to the weekend but that doesn't mean to say you will want to be stuck indoors. Looking at the needs of your partner is something you might choose to do today.

23 SUNDAY
Moon Age Day 20   Moon Sign Pisces

This is likely to be a business-as-usual sort of day. It doesn't lack potential but neither are you likely to find yourself pushing over any buses. You have to realise that you cannot be moving forward at full speed all the time. Contemplative days such as this have a greater importance than you sometimes realise.

24 MONDAY
Moon Age Day 21   Moon Sign Pisces

Don't rely entirely on your intuition today, despite the fact that it seems to be working strongly. You can still be fooled and may discover that a few people in your vicinity are not at all what you thought them to be. You also need to be aware that situations can change very quickly, which is a certain fact at the moment.

25 TUESDAY
Moon Age Day 22   Moon Sign Pisces

Stand by for a fairly hectic phase and one during which you have little or no time for the niceties of life. People will forgive you for being slightly off-hand, particularly since at least some of your efforts are geared in their direction. Concentrating on anything to do with family or friendship is virtually impossible.

26 WEDNESDAY
Moon Age Day 23   Moon Sign Aries

There is a tendency for you to be restless right now and that means filling your day with interesting diversions. The chances are that you are well up with practical tasks and you can probably afford to give some time to yourself. Keep away from any get-rich-quick schemes; they are very unlikely to work.

27 THURSDAY
Moon Age Day 24   Moon Sign Aries

When it comes to expressing yourself today, you are second to none. Conforming to expectations won't be easy but then it is the originality within your personality that appeals so much to others at present. You can get an audience, no matter what you choose to do. What's more, you relish being in the limelight.

28 FRIDAY
Moon Age Day 25   Moon Sign Taurus

Social and travel matters can keep you busy in equal proportions at the end of this working week. What will probably seem less interesting are the responsibilities of your everyday life. Trends reveal a tendency to shift your problems on to the shoulders of others, which is never the best way to proceed.

29 SATURDAY
Moon Age Day 26   Moon Sign Taurus

Personal freedom is important today but you can so easily feel fettered by circumstances. Find some way to prove to yourself that you are in charge of your own life and move away from situations that tie your hands for weeks or months to come. Give yourself some free time to simply do what pleases you.

30 SUNDAY
Moon Age Day 27   Moon Sign Gemini

You need to keep life as interesting and varied as you can. You can become bored very easily because you feel lazy but at the same time experience frustration if you are not getting ahead as you would wish. Simply show a little patience because circumstances are likely to change before very long.

July

2019

YOUR MONTH AT A GLANCE

⊕ = Opportunities are around   ⊖ = Be on the defensive   ⬤ = Life is pretty ordinary

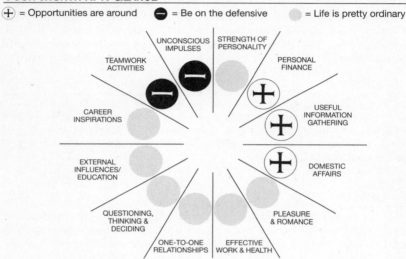

STRENGTH OF PERSONALITY

UNCONSCIOUS IMPULSES

TEAMWORK ACTIVITIES

PERSONAL FINANCE

CAREER INSPIRATIONS

USEFUL INFORMATION GATHERING

EXTERNAL INFLUENCES/ EDUCATION

DOMESTIC AFFAIRS

QUESTIONING, THINKING & DECIDING

PLEASURE & ROMANCE

ONE-TO-ONE RELATIONSHIPS

EFFECTIVE WORK & HEALTH

JULY HIGHS AND LOWS

Here I show you how the rhythms of the Moon will affect you this month. Like the tide, your energies and abilities will rise and fall with its pattern. When it is above the centre line, go for it, when it is below, you should be resting.

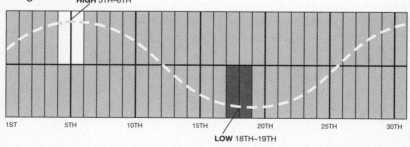

HIGH 5TH–6TH

1ST   5TH   10TH   15TH   20TH   25TH   30TH

LOW 18TH–19TH

84

I MONDAY
Moon Age Day 28   Moon Sign Gemini

You will enjoy a little more privacy today, in fact things being the way they are in the heavens you could more or less have the whole day to yourself. Sorting out things from the past is one of the options today, though it is clear that you should be casting your mind forward too. A good time to book a holiday.

2 TUESDAY
Moon Age Day 0   Moon Sign Gemini

Certain plans are now coming to fruition. The trouble is that now the time is here, you don't seem to have a great deal of personal choice regarding them. Make this a social day and one during which you find time to get out and about. It has to be said that this would be an excellent time for a summer break.

3 WEDNESDAY
Moon Age Day I   Moon Sign Cancer

Since work matters tend to be progressive and more or less looking after themselves, you are left to consider social and personal matters instead. The response you give to offers that are coming your way at this time is going to be quite important. Energy and determination appear to be going hand in hand for the moment.

4 THURSDAY
Moon Age Day 2   Moon Sign Cancer

It is at home you find yourself happiest now. There are some minor frustrations about but you tend to deal with these quickly and efficiently. If you find yourself facing something you really don't want to do, it might be best to tackle it very early in the day. At least that way there will be more moments to please yourself later.

5 FRIDAY
Moon Age Day 3   Moon Sign Leo

Both personal and professional objectives are worth chasing today, with the lunar high giving you staying power and a desire to get ahead. Your confidence is especially high and you may be turning your mind in the direction of love. For at least a few Leos this is the time for popping an important question.

6 SATURDAY
Moon Age Day 4   Moon Sign Leo

Your judgement in major decisions seems to be especially good right now and that is why you are able to take a chance or two that under normal circumstances you might not. Entertaining, bright, happy and charming, there is no doubt that you have the ability to turn a few heads, particularly in social outings tonight.

7 SUNDAY   *Moon Age Day 5   Moon Sign Virgo*

It is the small things of life that ought to be addressed today. Probably just as well because you are not exactly in the mood to take on anything major. Social functions ought to appeal and you may get the chance to get out into the fresh air. Family parties or informal functions could also be fun.

8 MONDAY   ☿   *Moon Age Day 6   Moon Sign Virgo*

You might not exactly create the state of disorganisation that exists around you today, but there is a chance you are contributing to it. Try to stay cool, calm and collected, even if you feel provoked. In particular it would be most sensible to avoid becoming involved in family disputes.

9 TUESDAY   ☿   *Moon Age Day 7   Moon Sign Libra*

You can get just as much from listening to others today as you can from contributing to situations yourself. In a practical sense you will now want to be ahead of the game and you could also discover a sporting attitude developing inside you. Try to vary life and take what you can from positive prevailing circumstances in love matches.

10 WEDNESDAY ☿   *Moon Age Day 8   Moon Sign Libra*

What you learn today can be of tremendous importance in the longer-term, which is why it is important to pay attention to what is being said in your immediate vicinity. There is a possibility of a new love interest coming into the lives of single Leos, together with a strengthening of ties for the rest.

11 THURSDAY   ☿   *Moon Age Day 9   Moon Sign Scorpio*

Romantically speaking there ought to be plenty of good things going on now. You enjoy being number one and that is the position that you are inclined to occupy in the mind of a number of people right now. Despite this fact, you cannot be everyone's cup of tea, a reality that you will have to accept, no matter how reluctantly.

12 FRIDAY   ☿   *Moon Age Day 10   Moon Sign Scorpio*

Today brings a slightly better period as far as your ego is concerned. Even casual contacts can now offer a degree of interest and perhaps potential success, particularly on the social scene. Try to avoid too much focus on professional matters on a day that will be better for relaxing and having fun.

13 SATURDAY ☿*Moon Age Day 11* *Moon Sign Sagittarius*

There are pleasant times to be had today, mainly because of the attitude you are taking towards life and the people you are meeting. With a cheerful smile you are able to counter any criticism that comes your way and you should discover that your general popularity is definitely on the increase.

14 SUNDAY ☿*Moon Age Day 12* *Moon Sign Sagittarius*

Though you remain generally optimistic, not everyone around you enjoys the same level of confidence. As a result, you will have to spend at least part of today convincing others that you know what you are talking about. Even if the going gets tough hang on in there. There are gains for Leos with staying power.

15 MONDAY ☿ *Moon Age Day 13* *Moon Sign Capricorn*

Focus on your love life as this new week begins. There is a good deal of ego fulfilment in the offing and so you notice that your popularity is particularly high. Making the right sort of decision should be easy, especially if you are willing to listen to the well-intentioned and quite sensible advice of friends.

16 TUESDAY ☿ *Moon Age Day 14* *Moon Sign Capricorn*

Right now you should be on the lookout for newcomers on the social scene. There are gains to be made financially, even if these prove to be of a fairly small nature. With restlessness in your spirit today it is very important that you spread yourself across a range of different interests.

17 WEDNESDAY ☿ *Moon Age Day 15* *Moon Sign Capricorn*

Favourable domestic relationships make it easier for you to concentrate on practical matters, without spending too much time sorting out the problems of your family. You won't be stuck for something to do socially, but there are times today when you could get bored with the same old routines.

18 THURSDAY ☿ *Moon Age Day 16* *Moon Sign Aquarius*

This is probably going to be a quiet day, but it can also be quite enjoyable. Not everyone you know may be being equally kind, though you are inclined to make excuses for one or two of them at present. Create a more comfortable space for yourself as the warmest weather approaches, perhaps in the garden.

19 FRIDAY ☿ *Moon Age Day 17 Moon Sign Aquarius*

Attend to little jobs today and don't try to push yourself too hard. You are quite creative at the moment and will want to beautify your surroundings. The slightly odd behaviour of others is something you have to cope with, even if it is more likely to make you laugh than to be annoyed.

20 SATURDAY ☿ *Moon Age Day 18 Moon Sign Pisces*

With more pressure noticeable at home, it is possible that younger family members give you some cause for concern. The attitude of friends could also be somewhat puzzling, which means having to ask some leading questions at some stage today. Keep abreast of events out there in the big, wide world.

21 SUNDAY ☿ *Moon Age Day 19 Moon Sign Pisces*

Success comes today if you are properly organised. Leaving situations to chance won't work half as well as preparing yourself for eventualities in advance and there is plenty of help around if you are willing to ask the right questions. Conforming to expectations could prove somewhat difficult later in the day.

22 MONDAY ☿ *Moon Age Day 20 Moon Sign Pisces*

It is likely that you will come across to others more forcefully than you intend at the moment. At the same time, you are creative and have a distinct flair when it comes to your looks and general attitude. This proves to be the right combination of attributes to get ahead at work and even to advance further than you expected.

23 TUESDAY ☿ *Moon Age Day 21 Moon Sign Aries*

Any recent delays are put aside and you reveal a tendency towards innovative thinking that really stands you in good stead. At the same time, you should be noticeably relaxed on the outside, even if you are shaking like a leaf inside. Avoid putting yourself through any more pressure than necessary.

24 WEDNESDAY ☿ *Moon Age Day 22 Moon Sign Aries*

This might be an excellent time for a proper change of scene. With the summer weather around and in the knowledge that you have bought yourself some time, you would be well advised to head for a high mountain or a very blue sea. If the pressure of work prevents a full holiday, opt for a short break.

25 THURSDAY ☿ *Moon Age Day 23   Moon Sign Taurus*

You will need to do things to please yourself today, even if that means upsetting someone else. One thing's for sure, and that's that you won't get very far by projecting all your concern towards others. Unless you are also contented with your lot, it is impossible for you to give your best. For this reason alone a little selfishness is necessary now.

26 FRIDAY ☿ *Moon Age Day 24   Moon Sign Taurus*

Since you are inclined to take yourself and your attributes very much for granted today, it probably isn't too surprising that you find other people doing the same thing. At least your creative potential is good and that means getting something looking just right at home or in the environment where you work.

27 SATURDAY ☿ *Moon Age Day 25   Moon Sign Taurus*

There is a powerful impulse to do things right and since your social conscience is very definitely sparked at this time, much of what you get through is on behalf of others. Energy is in abundance and the progressive qualities of the Lion are in your mind and showing in your actions.

28 SUNDAY ☿ *Moon Age Day 26   Moon Sign Gemini*

Patience is the watchword in money matters and this means keeping your purse or pocket tightly closed for now. There are better opportunities coming along soon, and in any case you don't need money in order to have a good time at the moment. Plan now for a period that can be both stimulating and different.

29 MONDAY ☿ *Moon Age Day 27   Moon Sign Gemini*

This is an excellent time to let the world know what a big personality you have. Stay away from those who seem to have it in their minds to cause difficulties for you, or at the very least refuse to rise to their bait. Concentrate on enjoying yourself and find ways to cheer up those who are less happy at present.

30 TUESDAY ☿ *Moon Age Day 28   Moon Sign Cancer*

Today could prove fairly good in terms of relationships and coming to terms with a colleague will probably turn out to be rather easier than you had imagined. Don't be too quick to jump to conclusions, particularly with regard to the way your lover is thinking and acting. There should be plenty of attention coming your way.

31 WEDNESDAY ☿

Moon Age Day 0   Moon Sign Cancer

Love life and social issues make for an interesting and even exciting midweek period. Although you might not get as much done as you would have wished, you can always catch up with jobs later. For now, go out and have a good time, probably in the company of your lover or relatives, rather than with friends.

2019

YOUR MONTH AT A GLANCE

$\oplus$ = Opportunities are around ● = Be on the defensive ◐ = Life is pretty ordinary

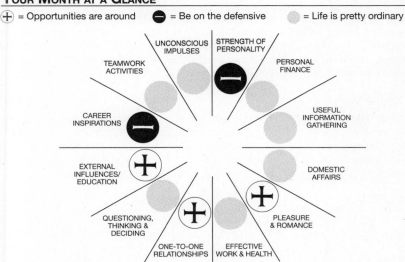

AUGUST HIGHS AND LOWS

Here I show you how the rhythms of the Moon will affect you this month. Like the tide, your energies and abilities will rise and fall with its pattern. When it is above the centre line, go for it, when it is below, you should be resting.

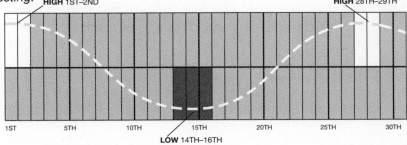

91

1 THURSDAY
Moon Age Day 1   Moon Sign Leo

In a holistic sense, this could turn out to be the very best day of the new month. It isn't only the lunar high that is working for you because a number of other planetary trends are also going your way. New ideas come into your mind all the time and your intuition is also particularly strong. You can afford to act on impulse.

2 FRIDAY
Moon Age Day 2   Moon Sign Leo

Have fun, that's what the stars are saying today. Most Leos will be in a holiday frame of mind, even if it isn't actually possible to get away at present. Be bold and ambitious because this shows in your attitude and actions. In turn, such behaviour is likely to attract the support and the positive attention of others.

3 SATURDAY
Moon Age Day 3   Moon Sign Virgo

Although you are going to great lengths to please others today, in a significant number of cases this could be a waste of energy. It will seem as though some people are quite unwilling to co-operate, no matter how much effort you put in. Don't be annoyed but simply switch your efforts in worthwhile directions instead.

4 SUNDAY
Moon Age Day 4   Moon Sign Virgo

Your tendency to be a little extravagant is obvious but it could have a bearing on your finances in the near future unless you exercise a little care. You can only wear so many clothes or own a finite number of possessions. If you stop to think about it, these considerations are not all that important anyway.

5 MONDAY
Moon Age Day 5   Moon Sign Libra

With a little gentle persuasion and the right attitude you can get more or less whatever you want from others today. This would be an ideal time for research of some sort, maybe in a library or on the internet. Communications of all sorts may bring rewarding news and some slight changes in your own attitude.

6 TUESDAY
Moon Age Day 6   Moon Sign Libra

You might be feeling good about family matters today, particularly those concerning something from the past that is replaying itself positively in your life at the moment. Although there are few hours in which you can simply have fun, the practical side of life appeals to you and may prove to be reward enough in itself.

7 WEDNESDAY — *Moon Age Day 7   Moon Sign Scorpio*

You are in a very optimistic frame of mind and willing to capitalise on this for all you are worth. There could be financial gains to be made in the middle of this week and you could make great headway at work. Don't be too pushy in social settings and allow situations to mature in their own good time.

8 THURSDAY — *Moon Age Day 8   Moon Sign Scorpio*

A sense of personal security might have you looking around your home and wondering how you can better protect what you have. That's fine, just as long as you do not become paranoid about anything. Stay away from new starts in practical matters, not because of the possibility of failure, but to spend more time with those you love.

9 FRIDAY — *Moon Age Day 9   Moon Sign Sagittarius*

Most of your energy will probably be piled into you work, though if you are still studying, or perhaps retired, you won't find it hard to fill your hours. Much of what you do is on behalf of others and almost all your tasks today will carry a special sort of satisfaction. Don't be surprised if people are saying nice things about you.

10 SATURDAY — *Moon Age Day 10   Moon Sign Sagittarius*

This is a good time for romance and a weekend that offers a number of wonderful incentives. Avoid anxiety over issues that really do not matter and concentrate on having fun. A long walk might be enjoyable, or, if the more materialistic side of your nature is on display, an enjoyable trip to the shops.

11 SUNDAY — *Moon Age Day 11   Moon Sign Sagittarius*

This could be one of the best periods of the month for financial gain, perhaps as a result of effort you have put in previously. You will probably be on the receiving end of gossip, but don't allow this to affect your opinions. The truth of any situation now lies is what you work out for yourself.

12 MONDAY — *Moon Age Day 12   Moon Sign Capricorn*

The emphasis moves away from the practical and towards the romantic. It looks as though you are now in a very good position to turn heads and to say the right words to impress others. However, not all of the attention you receive today will be as a result of your actions or turn out to be especially welcome.

13 TUESDAY
Moon Age Day 13   Moon Sign Capricorn

A non-stop period of talking is on the cards for Leo today. With plenty of cheek, especially at the times you need it most, a winning smile and a little of the blarney, who could resist you? You remain confident in your own ability to get what you want from life in a financial, or any material, sort of way.

14 WEDNESDAY
Moon Age Day 14   Moon Sign Aquarius

You should keep your life as free from complications as possible at present. The lunar low has come around and though it does little to depress you, it would be strange if you failed to notice that the going is somewhat tougher for the moment. Rely on close, personal ties because these suit you best now.

15 THURSDAY
Moon Age Day 15   Moon Sign Aquarius

Instant success will not be coming your way today. The lunar low holds back situations and makes it rather difficult for you to find the sort of progress you might wish. Use this as a contemplative period and a time when it is better to look ahead and plan, rather than to push forward in a direct sense.

16 FRIDAY
Moon Age Day 16   Moon Sign Aquarius

In terms of ideas, you should benefit from new input as the day advances. There is plenty to occupy your mind, in fact too much at times. You will definitely gain if you are willing to listen to the help and advice that comes from people who are in the know. Conforming to expectations can be difficult, though.

17 SATURDAY
Moon Age Day 17   Moon Sign Pisces

Your quick thinking could prove to be invaluable in matters associated with work. Others quite naturally turn to you for help or advice at present and you should have little difficulty controlling a number of events at the same time. Confidence grows as you discover just how many capabilities you possess.

18 SUNDAY
Moon Age Day 18   Moon Sign Pisces

Your efficiency is still well marked and because it is so obvious this is how you impress others. Although you might not advance in any tangible way right now, it is clear that someone is watching you. This is as relevant during your social time as it may be whilst you are engaged in your professional activities.

19 MONDAY

A certain issue could be causing some confusion to you right now, so it might be sensible to seek the advice of someone who has more experience than you. This is not an admission of failure on your part and is merely a sensible precaution. Matters of love continue to occupy your mind for at least part of the day.

20 TUESDAY

Any recent delays are having a knock-on effect and this means having to pace yourself at the start of today. Maybe when you have the time to think about things fully you will realise that much of what you are trying to do is duplication of effort. By the evening you might have convinced yourself to relax.

21 WEDNESDAY

This would be an excellent time for travel. Those Leos who have chosen to take a holiday right now have clearly made the right decision. You relish fresh places and new faces, so much so that there is a strong chance of making important new friends around now. Your confidence has rarely been higher.

22 THURSDAY

In professional matters you are moving ahead at a pace, leaving yourself with the feeling that progress is inevitable at this time. The more confidence you have, the greater is your potential for ultimate success. This may be the most progressive phase you have encountered at any time during this year so far.

23 FRIDAY

Take care that no impatient actions on your part upset the natural equilibrium of the day. There are some matters that are definitely best left the way they are, whilst interference will only cause difficulties. Half the time now you simply have to sit back and watch situations unfold.

24 SATURDAY

Things tend to turn out well on a material level, even if you don't have quite the same strength of personality that was the case recently. Don't worry about your limitations or you are sure to find them. Going for gold in sporting endeavours could boost your ego, though you may have to settle for silver.

25 SUNDAY
Moon Age Day 25   Moon Sign Gemini

You think swiftly and have no tendency to slow down. This might be something of a mistake because at least a few minutes spent today contemplating the results of your actions would be more than worthwhile. Keep an open mind about family issues and don't be too authoritarian with younger people.

26 MONDAY
Moon Age Day 26   Moon Sign Cancer

The current period is useful in terms of firming up securities and deciding what course of action would be best for the future. In many respects you are rather mellow at this time and more than anxious to show what you are capable of in terms of long-term, forward family planning. Seek the encouragement of your partner.

27 TUESDAY
Moon Age Day 27   Moon Sign Cancer

You can get much of your own way with others today, whilst at the same time convincing them that they are at the helm. Don't be too quick to jump to conclusions and be aware that not everything is quite what it might seem to be. Arguments in your vicinity are not your concern, so stay out of them.

28 WEDNESDAY
Moon Age Day 28   Moon Sign Leo

The lunar high arrives. Take all the ideas that have been sloshing about in your head and put them into practice. Enjoy the fact that others find you difficult to miss and keep talking. Singing your own praises might be tedious, if were not for the fact that you manage to do so in such a charming and entertaining way now.

29 THURSDAY
Moon Age Day 29   Moon Sign Leo

Putting just a little faith in Lady Luck is not a problem whilst the lunar high stays around. You need to feel fulfilled today and to be sure that you are heading in your own chosen direction. If this isn't the case, you will soon become discontented. Only the most extreme form of activity will satisfy you at the moment.

30 FRIDAY
Moon Age Day 0   Moon Sign Virgo

You can certainly make great strides at work, allowing you to prove yourself in areas that were not your forte before. It is quite possible that you will be strengthening your position at work and maybe looking at advancement. Even a total change of professional scene isn't entirely out of the question.

31 SATURDAY

This is not a day to concentrate on working issues. On the contrary, you want to go out and have fun. Finding people to join in should be far from difficult and it is clear that you are well liked and deeply respected. In terms of your own ego these factors prove to be extremely important.

Ω September
2019

YOUR MONTH AT A GLANCE

$\oplus$ = Opportunities are around $\ominus$ = Be on the defensive   = Life is pretty ordinary

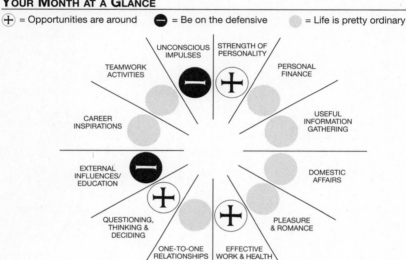

- UNCONSCIOUS IMPULSES
- STRENGTH OF PERSONALITY
- TEAMWORK ACTIVITIES
- PERSONAL FINANCE
- CAREER INSPIRATIONS
- USEFUL INFORMATION GATHERING
- EXTERNAL INFLUENCES/ EDUCATION
- DOMESTIC AFFAIRS
- QUESTIONING, THINKING & DECIDING
- PLEASURE & ROMANCE
- ONE-TO-ONE RELATIONSHIPS
- EFFECTIVE WORK & HEALTH

SEPTEMBER HIGHS AND LOWS

Here I show you how the rhythms of the Moon will affect you this month. Like the tide, your energies and abilities will rise and fall with its pattern. When it is above the centre line, go for it, when it is below, you should be resting.

HIGH 25TH–26TH

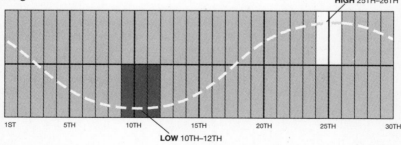

1ST   5TH   10TH   15TH   20TH   25TH   30TH

LOW 10TH–12TH

1 SUNDAY
Moon Age Day 2   Moon Sign Libra

There could be a few mistakes made today as a result of simple oversights on your part. That is why it is necessary to work slowly and steadily towards your objectives, without rushing or pushing. There is assistance around if you are willing to look for it, though being a Leo you probably will not.

2 MONDAY
Moon Age Day 3   Moon Sign Libra

It is towards work and practical matters that your mind is inclined to turn now. Routines can be rather boring because you want to break down fences and move forward progressively all the time. This isn't always possible and it is much more advisable on occasion to consolidate your position and to show patience.

3 TUESDAY
Moon Age Day 4   Moon Sign Scorpio

A little extra charm coming from your direction could go a long way in relationships this Tuesday. Not only can you make others happy, but you can also please yourself on the way. A partnership of some sort is getting stronger and results come in regarding efforts you have put in recently.

4 WEDNESDAY
Moon Age Day 5   Moon Sign Scorpio

Work progress should be fairly easy since you have just about all the support you could possibly need, and this is coming from a number of different directions. Of course not everyone is going to be on your side at the moment but when it really matters you should be able to find someone to back your hunches.

5 THURSDAY
Moon Age Day 6   Moon Sign Scorpio

You should now be well on top of necessary jobs and may even be willing to take a day off. Not that this means you will be idle. On the contrary, you could be in the market for a shopping spree, or for some even more robust sort of activity. Whatever you decide to do, make sure you are supporting other people too.

6 FRIDAY
Moon Age Day 7   Moon Sign Sagittarius

Although you could find yourself feeling rather restless at the moment, this is a state of affairs that you can counter with a little imagination. Enrol friends in some of your latest enterprises, get out and about when you are not at work, and do your best to cheer everyone up. That should give you plenty to do.

7 SATURDAY
Moon Age Day 8   Moon Sign Sagittarius

There is help coming from above today. No, you don't need to look to angelic help from some passing cloud because it is superiors and people in positions of influence who may offer you their support. Try not to get too involved in the arguments or discussions of other people. They can only cloud your horizons now.

8 SUNDAY
Moon Age Day 9   Moon Sign Capricorn

It is possible that you find circumstances now conspire to allow you a greater degree of personal freedom and self-choice. Grab the moment with both hands, despite the fact that this is Sunday. Even a very slight amount of pressure could convince others that your point of view is both measured and sensible.

9 MONDAY
Moon Age Day 10   Moon Sign Capricorn

A wonderfully romantic interlude is on the way. Those Leos who are not directly looking for love could find they are on the receiving end of affection in any case. Try not to do more than you have to early in the day, but by the time the late afternoon and evening come along you should be full of get-up-and-go.

10 TUESDAY
Moon Age Day 11   Moon Sign Aquarius

Your powers of vitality are taking something of a dive today. Because you have been galloping along so fast, the sudden brake applied by the lunar low is that much more noticeable. Don't be disheartened. Simply sit back and mull things over for a day or two. Everyone needs a rest, even irrepressible Leo.

11 WEDNESDAY
Moon Age Day 12   Moon Sign Aquarius

It might be sensible to put at least a few of your ideas on hold. Instead of dealing with the practicalities of life, spend some time with people you find interesting, and who have a positive view of you. Your ego needs massaging and what you definitely don't need at the moment are comments that belittle you in any way.

12 THURSDAY
Moon Age Day 13   Moon Sign Aquarius

The peace and quiet you may desire at home today probably won't be forthcoming. People want to visit you and may bring other friends with them. All in all, it could turn out to be an active sort of day. On the one hand you might complain about this, but being a Leo you should be pleased that life is eventful.

13 FRIDAY
Moon Age Day 14   Moon Sign Pisces

Partnerships of all sorts should prove smooth and co-operative around now. It doesn't matter whether these relate to business, or indeed to marriage. What matters is that you are getting on well with those around you and should find yourself able to expand your horizons into new and positive practical directions.

14 SATURDAY
Moon Age Day 15   Moon Sign Pisces

You could find you are heading for a more hectic time socially, possibly because of the arrival of the weekend. You haven't really put your feet up for some time and today appears to be no exception to this rule. Avoid too much fussing over issues that will sort themselves out if you only give them time.

15 SUNDAY
Moon Age Day 16   Moon Sign Aries

For the young or young-at-heart Leo the romantic possibilities of today are pronounced. It isn't so much what you feel for others today that counts, more the way you are able to put it into words. At work, you have been steaming ahead recently. Now it's time to play and the Lion manages that wonderfully.

16 MONDAY
Moon Age Day 17   Moon Sign Aries

A phase of high energy and significant output is now upon you. The Sun is positively placed, offering new incentives and the chance to get firmly ahead. Avoid involvement in family disputes, which will not be at all useful at such a generally busy and committed time.

17 TUESDAY
Moon Age Day 18   Moon Sign Aries

Making progress today is as dependent on others as on your own decisions. If colleagues or friends are not coming good with their promises, turn your attention in a different direction and be willing to modify your plans. Stay right away from boring routines in which you achieve next to nothing.

18 WEDNESDAY
Moon Age Day 19   Moon Sign Taurus

Normal service is resumed, after a day or two during which the problems of others may have fallen into your lap. This can be a busy and active midweek period and a time during which you will be wearing a number of different hats. Leos who are working today can get on especially well.

19 THURSDAY
Moon Age Day 20   Moon Sign Taurus

Professionally speaking, you are ready for just about any challenge that now comes your way. What will be less satisfying is dealing with day-to-day chores. Where possible, seek the help of someone who is better with routine work than you are. Leo wants to be in the driving seat at present.

20 FRIDAY
Moon Age Day 21   Moon Sign Gemini

Social groups and co-operative ventures have a great deal to offer you today, so much so that more practical considerations are likely to be taking a back seat. Your creative potential is strong and together with family members there is a strong chance that you want to make significant changes on the home front.

21 SATURDAY
Moon Age Day 22   Moon Sign Gemini

You could well afford to be a little bit ambitious right now, since your love affair with the more personal aspects of life is less enhanced under current trends. These switches in emphasis are not at all unusual for Leo and you respond to them in a very philosophical manner as, fortunately, do everyone else.

22 SUNDAY
Moon Age Day 23   Moon Sign Gemini

This is the best time for making new starts and for taking advantage of situations you see as being in your best interests. Don't take no for an answer, especially in a professional sense. September is, in any case, just about the best month of the year for getting what you want in a practical and financial way.

23 MONDAY
Moon Age Day 24   Moon Sign Cancer

Fortune favours the brave, which of course includes all Lions! Don't wait around to be invited to do anything today. Simply decide what you want from life and go out to get it. Some confidences may have to be kept, especially when they involve friends who have been a part of your life for years.

24 TUESDAY
Moon Age Day 25   Moon Sign Cancer

Personal relationships are good and offer a sense of 'rightness' that doesn't come from other spheres of your life. Sporting Leos ought to be in their element today and should be able to find ways to mix their physical exercise with professional demands. Don't be too quick to jump to any conclusion.

25 WEDNESDAY
Moon Age Day 26   Moon Sign Leo

Fresh starts are on the way and the lunar high offers you the best incentive this month to pitch in and have a go. This would be a great day for travel, or for putting across to others some of your best ideas. Confrontation should not be necessary, and in any case your razor sharp wit will avoid it.

26 THURSDAY
Moon Age Day 27   Moon Sign Leo

A physical and mental peak arrives for many sons and daughters of Leo. Keep up the pressure and let people know what you want from life. There are many occasions today when even strangers would lend a hand if they only knew what it was you are after. Your finances should strengthen, though you are spending wisely at present.

27 FRIDAY
Moon Age Day 28   Moon Sign Virgo

Be careful when it comes to making financial decisions because your mind is not working quite as sharply today as has been the case earlier in the month. It might be best to leave any large amounts of spending until a later date. For now, simply sit back and enjoy some of the good things of life.

28 SATURDAY
Moon Age Day 0   Moon Sign Virgo

New information is coming in all the time this weekend, though some of it won't be put to good use until later in the week. All the same, it's worth keeping your ears and eyes open because even apparent coincidences can turn out to be much more in the fullness of time. The attitude of a friend could be puzzling.

29 SUNDAY
Moon Age Day 1   Moon Sign Libra

Your personal charm is in evidence and the world isn't tardy when it comes to recognising this fact. It shouldn't be difficult to create the right impression and it should become obvious that you are doing well in the popularity stakes. Attitude is all-important, as you realise today.

30 MONDAY
Moon Age Day 2   Moon Sign Libra

Well-meaning emotional support from others isn't at all difficult to find, though whether or not you really want it is open to doubt. Try to stay cool about the situation and listen to what they have to say. After all, you don't have to take their advice and will most probably do what suits you best in any case.

October
2019

Your Month at a Glance

⊕ = Opportunities are around   ⊖ = Be on the defensive   ⬤ = Life is pretty ordinary

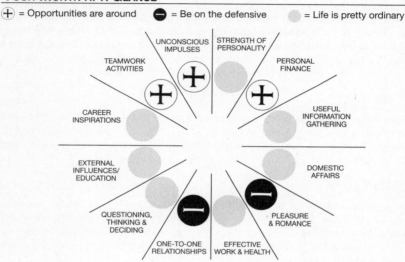

UNCONSCIOUS IMPULSES

STRENGTH OF PERSONALITY

TEAMWORK ACTIVITIES

PERSONAL FINANCE

CAREER INSPIRATIONS

USEFUL INFORMATION GATHERING

EXTERNAL INFLUENCES/ EDUCATION

DOMESTIC AFFAIRS

QUESTIONING, THINKING & DECIDING

PLEASURE & ROMANCE

ONE-TO-ONE RELATIONSHIPS

EFFECTIVE WORK & HEALTH

October Highs and Lows

Here I show you how the rhythms of the Moon will affect you this month. Like the tide, your energies and abilities will rise and fall with its pattern. When it is above the centre line, go for it, when it is below, you should be resting.

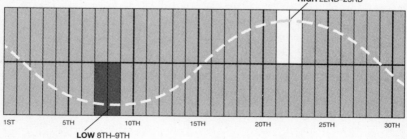

HIGH 22ND–23RD

1ST   5TH   10TH   15TH   20TH   25TH   30TH

LOW 8TH–9TH

1 TUESDAY
Moon Age Day 3   Moon Sign Scorpio

Minor tensions could be in evidence, particularly at home. You may decide it is better to spend more time with friends right now, taking the heat off domestic situations. At work you should be active and genuinely taking a chance when it proves to be most important to do so.

2 WEDNESDAY
Moon Age Day 4   Moon Sign Scorpio

The creative side of your nature is very much emphasised by prevailing planetary trends. Perhaps you are deciding to make changes in and around your home? If so, you should consult your partner. Other family members also have their part to play and it really is a case of being open to opinions now.

3 THURSDAY
Moon Age Day 5   Moon Sign Sagittarius

You are your own best public relations officer today. You are sensible, fearless and bold, yet at the same time caring and willing to listen. These really are the very best qualities of your zodiac sign and they are available for all to see. As a result you ought to find yourself on the receiving end of a very happy day.

4 FRIDAY
Moon Age Day 6   Moon Sign Sagittarius

Don't make life any more difficult than it needs to be by chasing up every detail or insisting on having your say. There are times right now when it would definitely be best to keep quiet, rather than to cause problems for yourself. The end of the working week could easily be marred with disputes, though you can avoid them if you are careful.

5 SATURDAY
Moon Age Day 7   Moon Sign Capricorn

Relationships tend to be rewarding today, which is why you may decide to drop most responsibilities and practical issues in favour of having fun. There are people around who make you laugh, and who are just as fond of you as you are of them. This is definitely not a day during which you need to complicate anything.

6 SUNDAY
Moon Age Day 8   Moon Sign Capricorn

New and enlivening experiences are just around the next corner. You may become a little frustrated that they don't turn up immediately, but that's the nature of Leo. Stay cool, calm and collected, even when you feel yourself provoked. If you do so there is a good chance you will break through any obstacle.

7 MONDAY
Moon Age Day 9   Moon Sign Capricorn

Socially speaking there are plenty of light-hearted and enjoyable moments highlighted in today's chart. Look out for new people coming into your life. They might not signify too much at the moment but it is only a matter of time before they begin to play a much more important part in your plans for the future.

8 TUESDAY
Moon Age Day 10   Moon Sign Aquarius

The information you receive from other people turns out to be both interesting and potentially helpful. For this reason alone it is worth keeping your ears open. Even gossip does not fall beneath your contempt for once, though of course being a Leo you certainly won't believe everything you hear.

9 WEDNESDAY
Moon Age Day 11   Moon Sign Aquarius

There is little assistance about for your plans today, though you probably did manage to get at least halfway through the lunar low without realising it was present. It would be best to keep a low profile for the moment, allowing others to take some of the strain and being willing to accept intervention and advice.

10 THURSDAY
Moon Age Day 12   Moon Sign Pisces

Don't be too obsessed with having everything perfectly organised today. A little disorganisation may even prove to be a blessing in disguise. You remain confident, though you could waver if you are faced with a brand new challenge of a sort that hasn't come your way before.

11 FRIDAY
Moon Age Day 13   Moon Sign Pisces

For some reason simple jobs seem to take twice the time today. That may not matter as much as it sometimes would, because it is the end of the working week after all. Plod along at your own pace, which should allow you to look around more than you usually do. The unexpected kindness of a friend may disarm you later in the day.

12 SATURDAY
Moon Age Day 14   Moon Sign Pisces

The weekend may see a specific loved one relying heavily on your judgement. This implies a high degree of responsibility but that is not an issue for the Lion. You will give the advice you know to be sensible and can be relied upon to offer good counsel and a great deal of natural sympathy.

13 SUNDAY
Moon Age Day 15   Moon Sign Aries

With Sunday comes a chance to enlist the help and co-operation of other people. It was inevitable right at the start of October that you would vacillate between listening and acting on impulse but today finds you very compliant. Sunday ought to offer good social prospects and a chance for new enterprises.

14 MONDAY
Moon Age Day 16   Moon Sign Aries

Career developments are helped by your capacity for hard work and your determination, which could be said to be legendary at the moment. You may still have to cope with a number of distractions that will thwart some of your intentions and test your patience once again. Friendships are very tight and secure today.

15 TUESDAY
Moon Age Day 17   Moon Sign Taurus

If anything, personal relationships might appear to be rather too intense today and you will want to actively lighten the load. Make room for the things other people are saying and don't turn down any advice that comes from reputable directions. Life can be tedious on occasions but not if you find ways to cut through red tape.

16 WEDNESDAY
Moon Age Day 18   Moon Sign Taurus

As the autumn winds begin to blow you might decide on one last trip before the end of the year. There are great opportunities about and it seems important at present to please yourself, though you might have to take the needs and wants of family members on board too.

17 THURSDAY
Moon Age Day 19   Moon Sign Taurus

An entire change of scene would certainly do you good and there are few issues that need resolving so badly that you can't take a break. You will benefit from coming back refreshed and better able to see the wood for the trees. Take special note of romantic proposals that come your way at or around this time.

18 FRIDAY
Moon Age Day 20   Moon Sign Gemini

Trends now benefit partnerships, whether they are of a practical, professional or a personal nature. Seeing the other person's point of view isn't always your strongpoint but is indicated by trends at present. Routines are for the birds this Friday and you insist on doing whatever comes into your mind.

19 SATURDAY
Moon Age Day 21   Moon Sign Gemini

Social affairs allow you to feel more carefree and to come to terms with your general popularity at the moment. Your attitude is good and the sense of humour you display at present is especially strong. There could be one or two things you don't want to do today and the simple advice is to get stuck in and sort them out quickly.

20 SUNDAY
Moon Age Day 22   Moon Sign Cancer

Time spent alone at the moment would be preferable to finding yourself at odds with others. Your concern for the underdog is strong but the necessary energy to do what it takes to sort matters out simply isn't present. This could also be a watershed moment in your thinking about career prospects in particular.

21 MONDAY
Moon Age Day 23   Moon Sign Cancer

This is an excellent time to look out anything unusual or even downright peculiar. Don't doubt your intuition at this stage because it is clearly strong and unlikely to lead you in the wrong direction. Counting on the support of a friend might be a mistake, if only because they are so busy and possibly quite worried at present.

22 TUESDAY
Moon Age Day 24   Moon Sign Leo

It's up and away now as the lunar high comes along, allowing you to live life to the full. You may find it possible to solve a problem that has been dogging you for quite some time and it ought to be quite clear that you enjoy great popularity now. Financially speaking you could find a boost coming your way.

23 WEDNESDAY
Moon Age Day 25   Moon Sign Leo

This is a superb time for putting new ideas into practice. Don't be held back by negative types and once you have made up your mind to go in any given direction, keep moving. Your social life should be a breeze and as your popularity increases there are new people joining the fan club.

24 THURSDAY
Moon Age Day 26   Moon Sign Virgo

Don't let good ideas languish today simply because you don't seem to have what it takes to make them work. Instead of taking no for an answer, push your weight around a little. This is not something that comes hard to Leo and could result in a positive listening ear from someone important.

25 FRIDAY
Moon Age Day 27   Moon Sign Virgo

The pace of events seems to slow a little, allowing you the time to pause and take breath. Because of the present astrological trends you are unlikely to think in terms of an extremely active day. On the contrary, the lure of a comfortable armchair might seem too irresistible to be ignored.

26 SATURDAY
Moon Age Day 28   Moon Sign Libra

You need to keep a variety of interests on the go now if at all possible. Don't be too quick to make dramatic changes, especially to your personal life. Today needs a gentle touch on the tiller and the certain knowledge that every action you take might have a slightly adverse bearing on others.

27 SUNDAY
Moon Age Day 0   Moon Sign Libra

You won't want to believe everything you hear today, but be cautious, because at least some of it will be true. Your confidence is growing all the time at work, but beware of being too clever for your own good. It is important to check and recheck all facts and figures before proceeding with any specific deal.

28 MONDAY
Moon Age Day 1   Moon Sign Scorpio

You could do worse than to stay close to those around you who have real power, particularly at work. Your own ideas are sound, and worth discussing with anyone who is willing to listen. Once work is out of the way, you will enjoy having a good time.

29 TUESDAY
Moon Age Day 2   Moon Sign Scorpio

A diverse range of interests may appeal to you close to the start of November. This would certainly seem to be what the present planetary line-up is indicating. However, there are specific issues that are presently difficult to avoid. Turning your attention towards them won't be too appealing, but could be necessary.

30 WEDNESDAY
Moon Age Day 3   Moon Sign Sagittarius

There are some good ideas on the financial front and you will need to implement them just as quickly as you can. This is an ideal time for taking any problem by the scruff of the neck and shaking it into order. Don't take no for an answer, particularly from someone you have the power to override gently.

31 THURSDAY

Moon Age Day 4   Moon Sign Sagittarius

Others are looking upon you very favourably now and are not likely to cause you any undue problems. If they have influence, so much the better. Be as sensitive as possible at home in order to avoid accidentally overruling a relative who is genuinely doing their best.

November
2019

YOUR MONTH AT A GLANCE

⊕ = Opportunities are around   ⊖ = Be on the defensive   ⬤ = Life is pretty ordinary

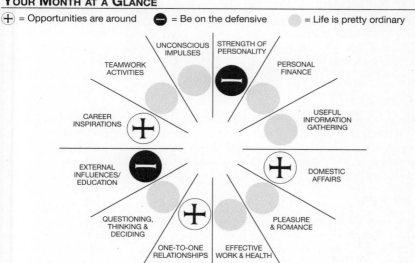

- UNCONSCIOUS IMPULSES
- STRENGTH OF PERSONALITY
- TEAMWORK ACTIVITIES
- PERSONAL FINANCE
- CAREER INSPIRATIONS
- USEFUL INFORMATION GATHERING
- EXTERNAL INFLUENCES/ EDUCATION
- DOMESTIC AFFAIRS
- QUESTIONING, THINKING & DECIDING
- PLEASURE & ROMANCE
- ONE-TO-ONE RELATIONSHIPS
- EFFECTIVE WORK & HEALTH

NOVEMBER HIGHS AND LOWS

Here I show you how the rhythms of the Moon will affect you this month. Like the tide, your energies and abilities will rise and fall with its pattern. When it is above the centre line, go for it, when it is below, you should be resting.

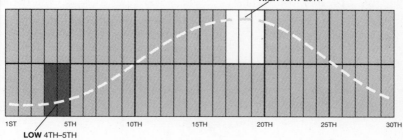

HIGH 18TH–20TH

1ST   5TH   10TH   15TH   20TH   25TH   30TH

LOW 4TH–5TH

1 FRIDAY ☿   *Moon Age Day 5   Moon Sign Sagittarius*

There are influences about now that keep you in touch with people you may not see all that often. Your mind tends to travel back as much as it is pushed forward and you have a great deal to think about in professional terms. This may turn out to be quite a busy day, though it is diverse and, in most cases, interesting.

2 SATURDAY ☿   *Moon Age Day 6   Moon Sign Capricorn*

This might be quite a demanding day, albeit in a low-key sort of way. You move from one situation to another that each demand your full attention and there won't be quite the level of rest and relaxation you might wish. There is a forward push on your part to sweep away cobwebs and to see new possibilities.

3 SUNDAY ☿   *Moon Age Day 7   Moon Sign Capricorn*

Getting out and about socially may be just what you need to keep a smile on your face today. Too much commitment to practical matters could prove boring and you will feel much happier with some variety in your life. Romantic issues might be on your mind later in the day. Your confidence is reasonably high.

4 MONDAY ☿   *Moon Age Day 8   Moon Sign Aquarius*

There are some limitations to be faced today and tomorrow. This is more or less entirely due to the lunar low and there probably isn't much you can do about it. Instead of bemoaning the fact, enjoy some rest and relaxation. There is no barrier to having fun, especially when this is of a low-key sort.

5 TUESDAY ☿   *Moon Age Day 9   Moon Sign Aquarius*

Don't take any big risks today. Be willing to settle for a peaceful life and allow others to do the hard work. You are undergoing sea-changes in thinking at the moment and it won't do any harm for you to have some moments for reflection. In reality, you should get a good deal more done right now than you expect.

6 WEDNESDAY ☿   *Moon Age Day 10   Moon Sign Pisces*

Some of the personal changes that are going on in your life at the moment need looking at very carefully. It is possible that you are being forced down paths you don't really want to follow. Friends will be on your side in minor disputes but it would be better to avoid these altogether if possible.

7 THURSDAY ☿ *Moon Age Day 11   Moon Sign Pisces*

Career matters seem to be a test of your patience today but your responsibility to work may not extend into the evening. Whatever time you do have to call your own, spend it in the company of people who interest you. Do a little questioning if you want to get to the bottom of a specific issue.

8 FRIDAY ☿ *Moon Age Day 12   Moon Sign Pisces*

This should be a lovely time for all intimate matters. Quite a few planetary indicators are suggesting that love is in the air, together with friendship and a feeling of togetherness. Any hard edge to Leo certainly isn't on display at this time and it is likely that certain people will realise what an old pussycat you really are.

9 SATURDAY ☿ *Moon Age Day 13   Moon Sign Aries*

Minor challenges in domestic issues probably cannot be avoided, that is if you stay around at home too much. It would be very easy to become bored during the first part of this weekend. By tomorrow you are on top form again but for the moment you could do with getting some variety into your life.

10 SUNDAY ☿ *Moon Age Day 14 · Moon Sign Aries*

You can't get by without a few ups and downs, even though one or two of them will be completely unexpected. You appear to be equal to almost any task that comes your way right now and you can also call on the support of relatives and friends, all of whom are happy to be of service now.

11 MONDAY ☿ *Moon Age Day 15   Moon Sign Taurus*

There is now a chance to firm up life in the monetary stakes. With better organisation and planning, backed up by a genuine intuition, you should be taking all the right decisions. Think through any strategy that involves levelling with family members. You need to be diplomatic, yet still get your message across.

12 TUESDAY ☿ *Moon Age Day 16   Moon Sign Taurus*

You can be very motivated in the creative stakes today. It could be that you are making changes around house and home, or perhaps getting involved in some new hobby or pastime. Don't spend too much time doing practical things today. The astrological picture shows that you really do need to have fun too.

13 WEDNESDAY ☿
Moon Age Day 17   Moon Sign Taurus

The value of self-reliance and independence is evident for the sign of the Lion today. All in all you are in for a fairly positive time. You can't expect everyone to like you but at least you have it within you now to ignore the people who do not. Getting to your chosen objectives ought to be a piece of cake.

14 THURSDAY ☿
Moon Age Day 18   Moon Sign Gemini

Travel should prove to be highly pleasurable, even though this may not be the best part of the year weather-wise. At any rate you need a change of scenery. Those Leos who are able to take a winter holiday would certainly enjoy getting away now. Consideration for other people appears to be high.

15 FRIDAY ☿
Moon Age Day 19   Moon Sign Gemini

Look out for a refreshing change of scene. It is true that these trends may have turned up one day too early for many Leos, but even if you only get an hour or two's diversion you should enjoy the change. An evening shop or an impromptu social function would work well. Seek out good friends today.

16 SATURDAY ☿
Moon Age Day 20   Moon Sign Cancer

A period of transformation is upon you and this is a long-term affair with quite far-reaching implications. It won't be until December that you fully appreciate some of the opportunities now developing in your life. Avoid arguments on a personal level and simply get on with what is expected of you.

17 SUNDAY ☿
Moon Age Day 21   Moon Sign Cancer

Now you look likely to be on a personal voyage of discovery, so don't be surprised if some facts and figures come in that give you a greater understanding of the way the world works. With a renewed sense of wonder and plenty of incentive, it looks as though today could be rather special, if somewhat unusual.

18 MONDAY ☿
Moon Age Day 22   Moon Sign Leo

Press ahead with all major plans and don't allow yourself to be held back when you can see that the going is good. There ought to be plenty to occupy your mind and your body today, with the start of a new working week likely to be bringing forth new possibilities of both a professional and a personal nature.

19 TUESDAY ☿   *Moon Age Day 23   Moon Sign Leo*

This would be a good time to put your luck to the test. Although you certainly won't want to put all your available cash on the next horse running, you can take calculated financial risks with better than average expectations of success. Physically and mentally most Leos should now be doing well.

20 WEDNESDAY ☿   *Moon Age Day 24   Moon Sign Leo*

This could prove to be one of the best days of November when it comes to career interests. However, you do need to take care to diversify when necessary and should not allow yourself to get stuck in any sort of rut. Listen to some sound professional advice from someone in the know.

21 THURSDAY   *Moon Age Day 25   Moon Sign Virgo*

There is a great deal of help on offer when it comes to professional developments. All the same, you will also be quite occupied with home-based issues and might have to spend a part of the day convincing family members that your point of view is the most valid. Don't be too quick to take offence in simple discussions.

22 FRIDAY   *Moon Age Day 26   Moon Sign Virgo*

News from far off should prove to be a good stimulus to your personal life. Perhaps someone you haven't heard from for ages is getting in touch again, offering you a journey or planning one? At work you need to show a very positive face to new incentives, even if you have doubts about them.

23 SATURDAY   *Moon Age Day 27   Moon Sign Libra*

This is an ideal time to decide whether you should jettison some aspects of life that are now of little or no use to you. Concentrate on the matter at hand, even though this is going to be quite difficult. When the practicalities are out of the way, make the most of very favourable social and romantic trends.

24 SUNDAY   *Moon Age Day 28   Moon Sign Libra*

This is a Sunday and so it wouldn't be surprising if you were to find yourself in the bosom of your family. You should feel partly pleased about this, though there is still a burning desire inside you to address issues that are less likely to be resolved at the weekend. Try to be patient and enjoy family times.

25 MONDAY
Moon Age Day 29   Moon Sign Scorpio

You may be too busy to worry much about money in a day-to-day sense and yet it is very important to do so. Those Leos who take a responsible attitude to life will already be planning for Christmas and today would be fine for shopping or for looking carefully at exactly what is available to spend.

26 TUESDAY
Moon Age Day 0   Moon Sign Scorpio

You can expect a day of satisfactory accomplishments, even if situations are not as clear-cut as you might wish. Getting to the nitty-gritty of specific matters won't be easy but you do have it in your power to show a determined and positive face to issues that you know are going to be important later.

27 WEDNESDAY
Moon Age Day 1   Moon Sign Sagittarius

A matter between yourself and a loved one today can have a strong bearing on your ability to enjoy yourself. Pay close attention to emotional issues because they could turn out to be more important than you think. Friends can be of great importance in the days ahead and you will be addressing their needs and wants.

28 THURSDAY
Moon Age Day 2   Moon Sign Sagittarius

It is time to explore the big, wide world beyond your own front door. Although it is late in the year you might opt for travel or for some other diversion that is a million miles away from the everyday considerations of your life. Your roving mind may make it difficult to concentrate on some issues at the moment.

29 FRIDAY
Moon Age Day 3   Moon Sign Capricorn

There now seems to be a strong accent on physical pleasures, though you are not about to slacken your efforts with regard to work. Loving relationships are quite obvious as places of resort once the working day is over but you could find certain family members behaving in a less than typical way.

30 SATURDAY
Moon Age Day 4   Moon Sign Capricorn

What seems to matter more than almost anything today is a strong sense of security. This could take many forms, from adding extra bolts to the door, right through to examining your insurance policies. Much of this seems tedious but you are in the right frame of mind to address such issues on this late November Saturday.

♌

December

2019

YOUR MONTH AT A GLANCE

⊕ = Opportunities are around ⊖ = Be on the defensive ● = Life is pretty ordinary

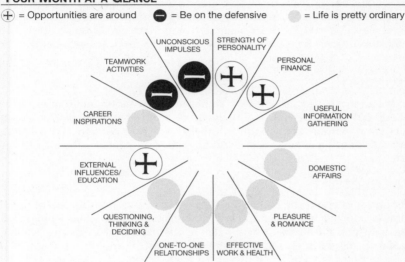

UNCONSCIOUS IMPULSES

STRENGTH OF PERSONALITY

TEAMWORK ACTIVITIES

PERSONAL FINANCE

CAREER INSPIRATIONS

USEFUL INFORMATION GATHERING

EXTERNAL INFLUENCES/ EDUCATION

DOMESTIC AFFAIRS

QUESTIONING, THINKING & DECIDING

PLEASURE & ROMANCE

ONE-TO-ONE RELATIONSHIPS

EFFECTIVE WORK & HEALTH

DECEMBER HIGHS AND LOWS

Here I show you how the rhythms of the Moon will affect you this month. Like the tide, your energies and abilities will rise and fall with its pattern. When it is above the centre line, go for it, when it is below, you should be resting.

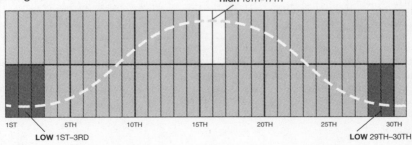

HIGH 16TH–17TH

1ST   5TH   10TH   15TH   20TH   25TH   30TH

LOW 1ST–3RD

LOW 29TH–30TH

1 SUNDAY
Moon Age Day 5   Moon Sign Aquarius

If you can avoid doing too much work today then so much the better. The lunar low makes you lethargic and much more willing than usual to put your feet up. Keep a low profile socially too, maybe settling for spending some hours on your own. At least the rest should do you good.

2 MONDAY
Moon Age Day 6   Moon Sign Aquarius

This should be another reasonably quiet day. For those Leos who already have their Christmas heads on, this might be a good period to look ahead and to plan. This ought to be a slightly better day on the social front and romance is around for those of you who want to make yourselves available to greet it.

3 TUESDAY
Moon Age Day 7   Moon Sign Aquarius

You are aware that give and take is important today and you are unlikely to lose sight of that fact. You might have to be somewhat devious if you want to get your own way and yet still let others know how committed you are to them. Don't tell any lies, even if you have to be somewhat liberal with the truth.

4 WEDNESDAY
Moon Age Day 8   Moon Sign Pisces

Although you could find there are one or two professional setbacks to be addressed, in the main you are still progressive, hopeful and aspirational. Turn your mind away from work later in the day towards fun and games, which become an increasing part of your life as the month advances. You remain in a strongly confident mood.

5 THURSDAY
Moon Age Day 9   Moon Sign Pisces

There are others to contend with today, one or two of whom are anxious for you to follow their lead. To do so probably won't appeal and the difficulty comes in letting them know this without inadvertently offering offence. A little mistake made early in the day should be easy to put right later.

6 FRIDAY
Moon Age Day 10   Moon Sign Aries

Along comes a brand new influence, increasing your desire for new experiences and causing you to willingly throw over traditions and routines. This is fine for you, but with Christmas only just around the corner you have to respect the fact that some people close to you want to leave things the way they are.

7 SATURDAY
Moon Age Day 11   Moon Sign Aries

This is a time to be seeking wide, open spaces. The weekend offers a sense of freedom and the chance to do something different. What you wouldn't take kindly to right now is being restricted in any way. There are plenty of people around you who would be only too pleased to join you on a flight of fancy.

8 SUNDAY
Moon Age Day 12   Moon Sign Aries

Your best areas at the moment come through travel, mental exercise of almost any sort and through simple human contact. Still friendly, and very anxious to help wherever you can, you seek out good causes and do your best to get the rest of the world into the same Christmas spirit that you presently feel.

9 MONDAY
Moon Age Day 13   Moon Sign Taurus

Don't be influenced by over-emotional states that come along today. You may not be in quite the same party mood that was the case a few days ago but you can still have fun. A good dose of fresh air would undoubtedly do you good, so don't stay glued to the television set in your free hours.

10 TUESDAY
Moon Age Day 14   Moon Sign Taurus

Your social life ought to prove quite rewarding. Your creative potential is also good and you may have decided to make some sort of change at home. As long as it is something that makes you more comfortable and not less so, your efforts are worthwhile! Sit back and let someone else undertake a domestic task.

11 WEDNESDAY
Moon Age Day 15   Moon Sign Gemini

There could be much about today that will make you feel generally happy and contented with your lot in life. You seem to have temporarily shelved your accustomed need to get ahead at all costs in favour of sitting back and relaxing whilst surveying your accomplishments so far this year.

12 THURSDAY
Moon Age Day 16   Moon Sign Gemini

Do keep your life as varied as you can and don't be too tied to issues that are of no real importance. It isn't hard for you to cherry-pick at present, opting for those aspects of life that hold a genuine fascination for you. Some confusion regarding social or travel details can soon be sorted out.

13 FRIDAY
Moon Age Day 17   Moon Sign Cancer

Influences coming your way in a career sense are much to the fore. Little things you hear play on your mind and cause you to look carefully at half-forgotten matters or ones that didn't look important before. Intuition is strong and ought to tell you when a potential purchase is really worth the asking price.

14 SATURDAY
Moon Age Day 18   Moon Sign Cancer

There are financial challenges around at the moment and these must be addressed very carefully. Perhaps you have been taking certain matters for granted but you won't be able to do so right now. Caution is the keyword, something that is sometimes difficult for your zodiac sign to address.

15 SUNDAY
Moon Age Day 19   Moon Sign Cancer

Put domestic issues into focus, even if this means ignoring some of the more practical issues of life for a while. Christmas is just around the corner and you won't get away with shelving any personal issue. Conforming to the patterns others set for you is probably easier than would normally be the case.

16 MONDAY
Moon Age Day 20   Moon Sign Leo

This is the best part of the month when it comes to having the necessary get-up-and-go to really change your life and its circumstances. With a good deal of empathy, and a great desire to please others, there is no reason at all why you should ruffle any feathers. Life is hectic, but it can be settled too.

17 TUESDAY
Moon Age Day 21   Moon Sign Leo

This is another day on which you should have plenty to say for yourself and no shortage of energy with which to get things done. Creature comforts are not all that important to you at the moment and you are quite prepared to go through some discomfort in order to achieve your objectives. You are also extremely friendly today.

18 WEDNESDAY
Moon Age Day 22   Moon Sign Virgo

Practical matters are likely to turn out the way you would wish. Last minute planning and preparations should go well, but you could be slightly bothered by the attitude of friends, which seems odd. Family members may be pestering you all the time, especially younger people, but this probably won't be a problem to you.

19 THURSDAY
Moon Age Day 23   Moon Sign Virgo

The greatest successes at the moment are likely to come in terms of your professional life and practical matters generally. Instead of insisting that you need do your own thing, be willing to compromise. Look out for the odd lucky break and use it to the full.

20 FRIDAY
Moon Age Day 24   Moon Sign Libra

This is a period during which you have high spirits and energy to spare. You find yourself in a good period to push for what you want, even though some of the plans you are laying down will not mature for another year or so. Combining your efforts with those who think the way you do could prove to be sensible.

21 SATURDAY
Moon Age Day 25   Moon Sign Libra

There can something distinctly odd but also amazing about the forthcoming Christmas period, though not in a difficult sense. Out-of-the-ordinary experiences are likely, together with messages from people you may not have been in contact with for ages. All in all, today is a good day for communicating with others and for enjoying their antics.

22 SUNDAY
Moon Age Day 26   Moon Sign Scorpio

Places of entertainment are now right up your street, which is probably just as well bearing in mind the time of year and the season. You can get by on very little when it comes to food and drink, so too much indulgence won't appeal to you around now. What you do relish is being in the social limelight.

23 MONDAY
Moon Age Day 27   Moon Sign Scorpio

Life becomes even more interesting and there is little time for circumspection. You find yourself to be very much a creature of the moment and won't have too many hours to spend meditating. Reacting in a moment-by-moment sense is what makes Leo tick, so such trends are no problem to you.

24 TUESDAY
Moon Age Day 28   Moon Sign Sagittarius

Airing the way you feel can sometimes be uncomfortable if you are a Leo, but trends suggest that you may be doing just that today. The position of the Moon inclines you to spill the beans and you might become quite emotional as a result. Christmas Eve should be generally happy, though.

25 WEDNESDAY
Moon Age Day 29   Moon Sign Sagittarius

Friendship-wise, a continuing influence shows itself whereby your world becomes ever more pleasant and fulfilling. This is just as well, because Christmas Day might have some restrictions and bolstering yourself against them now is worthwhile. Keep an open mind regarding the peculiar behaviour of some family members.

26 THURSDAY
Moon Age Day 0   Moon Sign Capricorn

Everyday obligations can now be a cause of some frustration. This situation can be mitigated if you allow others to take some of the strain. Delegating any facet of your life is not easy but is a lesson worth learning because it prevents you from becoming too fatigued. Avoid family arguments at all costs.

27 FRIDAY
Moon Age Day 1   Moon Sign Capricorn

You may learn something new and exciting now. Keep your eyes open and be willing to alter your plans at the last minute in order to achieve something splendid. It's turning out to be a hectic and effective period between Christmas and New Year but don't forget that part of the reason for holidays is to have a rest.

28 SATURDAY
Moon Age Day 2   Moon Sign Capricorn

Social matters, and friendships especially, should prove to be extremely rewarding at this time. Although you won't get through jobs quite as quickly or easily as you might have hoped, you will get where you want to be eventually. Happiness follows you throughout most of the day, together with a feeling of contentment.

29 SUNDAY
Moon Age Day 3   Moon Sign Aquarius

It has to be said from the start that a relaxing day would suit you best of all. For once you will be quite happy to sit back and watch everyone else continue the celebrations. Family trends are especially strong and some of the restless qualities of Leo are now definitely shelved.

30 MONDAY
Moon Age Day 4   Moon Sign Aquarius

You are still not too anxious to push yourself forward or to live the high life. Those around you might be surprised at your tendency to avoid too much to drink or a lot of rich food. Still, you should be content and happy with your lot and will be in a position to offer much support to family members and friends.

31 TUESDAY

Moon Age Day 5   Moon Sign Pisces

You will want to be noticed on this New Year's Eve and may go to great lengths to make sure you are not ignored by anyone. Beware of alienating others by taking an attitude they can't understand. Your resolutions for the year ahead could well include a determination to push your practical capabilities to the full.

How to Calculate Your Rising Sign

Most astrologers agree that, next to the Sun Sign, the most important influence on any person is the Rising Sign at the time of their birth. The Rising Sign represents the astrological sign that was rising over the eastern horizon when each and every one of us came into the world. It is sometimes also called the Ascendant.

Let us suppose, for example, that you were born with the Sun in the zodiac sign of Libra. This would bestow certain characteristics on you that are likely to be shared by all other Librans. However, a Libran with Aries Rising would show a very different attitude towards life, and of course relationships, than a Libran with Pisces Rising.

For these reasons, this book shows how your zodiac Rising Sign has a bearing on all the possible positions of the Sun at birth. Simply look through the Aries table opposite.

As long as you know your approximate time of birth the graph will show you how to discover your Rising Sign.

Look across the top of the graph of your zodiac sign to find your date of birth, and down the side for your birth time (I have used Greenwich Mean Time). Where they cross is your Rising Sign. Don't forget to subtract an hour (or two) if appropriate for Summer Time.

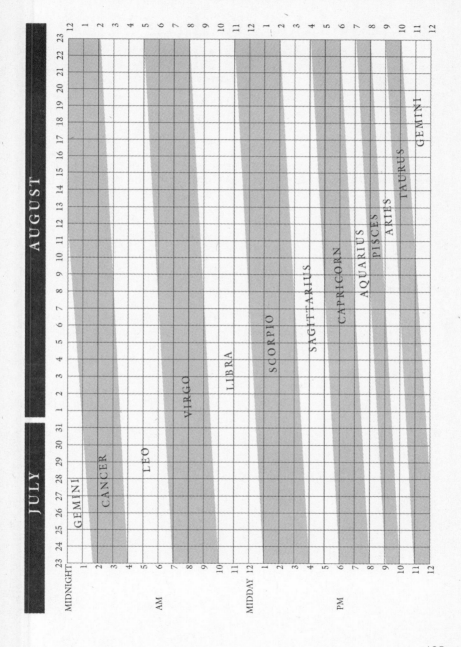

THE ZODIAC, PLANETS AND CORRESPONDENCES

The Earth revolves around the Sun once every calendar year, so when viewed from Earth the Sun appears in a different part of the sky as the year progresses. In astrology, these parts of the sky are divided into the signs of the zodiac and this means that the signs are organised in a circle. The circle begins with Aries and ends with Pisces.

Taking the zodiac sign as a starting point, astrologers then work with all the positions of planets, stars and many other factors to calculate horoscopes and birth charts and tell us what the stars have in store for us.

The table below shows the planets and Elements for each of the signs of the zodiac. Each sign belongs to one of the four Elements: Fire, Air, Earth or Water. Fire signs are creative and enthusiastic; Air signs are mentally active and thoughtful; Earth signs are constructive and practical; Water signs are emotional and have strong feelings.

It also shows the metals and gemstones associated with, or corresponding with, each sign. The correspondence is made when a metal or stone possesses properties that are held in common with a particular sign of the zodiac.

Finally, the table shows the opposite of each star sign – this is the opposite sign in the astrological circle.

Placed	Sign	Symbol	Element	Planet	Metal	Stone	Opposite
1	Aries	Ram	Fire	Mars	Iron	Bloodstone	Libra
2	Taurus	Bull	Earth	Venus	Copper	Sapphire	Scorpio
3	Gemini	Twins	Air	Mercury	Mercury	Tiger's Eye	Sagittarius
4	Cancer	Crab	Water	Moon	Silver	Pearl	Capricorn
5	Leo	Lion	Fire	Sun	Gold	Ruby	Aquarius
6	Virgo	Maiden	Earth	Mercury	Mercury	Sardonyx	Pisces
7	Libra	Scales	Air	Venus	Copper	Sapphire	Aries
8	Scorpio	Scorpion	Water	Pluto	Plutonium	Jasper	Taurus
9	Sagittarius	Archer	Fire	Jupiter	Tin	Topaz	Gemini
10	Capricorn	Goat	Earth	Saturn	Lead	Black Onyx	Cancer
11	Aquarius	Waterbearer	Air	Uranus	Uranium	Amethyst	Leo
12	Pisces	Fishes	Water	Neptune	Tin	Moonstone	Virgo